New Jersey's Best Shopping

To my late Grandmother, Lil,
the Shopper of the
Western World

About the Author

Liz Fuerst has been a newspaper reporter,
magazine editor, and arts critic. She has her own
public relations firm, First to Know Communications,
in Somerville, New Jersey and teaches journalism
at Rutgers University, New Brunswick. Shopping is
her passion. So is poking around the nooks and
crannies of New Jersey. This book is the
result of following both muses.

Golden Sun Books
A division of PDQ Press, Inc.
P.O. Box 715

Princeton Junction, New Jersey   08550
Copyright © 1998 by Golden Sun Books
ISBN: 0-9637022-4-6
Designed by Sue Bannon

Special Sales

Bulk purchases (10 copies or more) of
Golden Sun Books **New Jersey's Best** guides are
available to corporations, organizations, mail-order
catalogs, institutions, and charities at special discounts.
For more information write or call Golden Sun
Books at: P.O. Box 715, Princeton Junction,
New Jersey 08550; phone:(609)799-2800;
fax:(609)799-2802.
email: PDQ8@aol.com

New, Jersey's Best Shopping

**Dozens of Day Trips for the
Passionate Shopper**

CONTENTS

NORTHERN NEW JERSEY

CENTRAL NEW JERSEY

SOUTHERN NEW JERSEY

INTRODUCTION

The way New Jerseyans shop has changed, with malls replacing Main Streets and people viewing shopping as a recreational activity rather than a chore. The catalyst for the change has been the loss of leisure time. We are working longer hours, tending house and garden, performing community service, and participating in sports and activities that keep us and our children physically fit.

Rarely can we steal away to find that perfect outfit or buy that present for a gracious host and hostess. We resort to catalogs and home shopping by television, an efficient but oddly unsatisfying form of shopping. Had we the time, most of us would prefer to feel the rustle of silken fabric or observe how a piece of silver jewelry gleams on our wrists.

So we save up our free moments like pennies in a piggy bank, and when we collect a chunk of leisure time, we are ready to let loose. New Jerseyans often like to spend this time shopping, dining, sightseeing, and going to the movies – preferably in one place or town.

And that is why I wrote this book. I wanted to tell readers about destinations in our state that are worth a whole day of foot patrol. I wanted to inform you not only about shopping opportunities but also about small, out-of-the-way restaurants, interesting sites of historic and cultural interest, and magnificent countryside.

I wanted you to experience the length and breadth of New Jersey as I have done, first as a child touring with my family, then as a newspaper reporter, travel writer, and parent.

I wanted you to know there are communities in the Garden State as engaging as any Provençal village featured in the *Guide Michelin*. And with shops as exciting as Fifth Avenue and Rodeo Drive!

Every destination in the book is grouped according to region – Northern, Central, and Southern

Jersey — so you can concentrate on trips closer to home or spread your wings. Telephone numbers are included so if you have any question at all that a shop might be open (particularly true with antiques shops), call ahead.

May you have many happy hours of hunting and gathering.

Liz Fuerst

HOW TO USE THIS BOOK

Depending on whether you want to shop close to home or adventure far afield, *New Jersey's Best Shopping* divides its destinations by northern, central, and southern zones.

Once you've determined your destination, you will find each entry is standardized.

An introduction gives you an overview of the destination, its picturesque areas, and historical or recreational sites.

The **Directions** section tells you how to get there from the major roads that criss-cross New Jersey.

Strategies helps you best plan your day — where to park or when to walk instead of drive.

Best Shopping is the heart of the book. It lists the stores you'll want to visit, but remember listings are only a guide. While shopping a destination, you most assuredly will see other stores that appeal to you. Take the time to go in and make your own discoveries. Each shop listing contains a store's address (cross streets or other locator hints are given when helpful) and telephone number. Shop hours are included only when they are unusual, so if you have any question about opening and closing, do not hesitate to telephone. Some stores are part of chains, especially those in outlet malls, and may be listed in several destinations. In that instance, there is one principal description and the reader is referred back to that.

Under **Eats and Tasty Takeout,** you will find restaurants and gourmet takeout food shops. The restaurants were selected primarily because they serve a delightful lunch. However, most serve dinner, should you want to shop late. The listing tells you whether a particular restaurant is informal or fancy, inexpensive or expensive. The gourmet takeout food shops are where you can stop at the end of your day and buy mouth-watering meals to take home. After a day of shopping, who wants to cook?

Under **Worth A Detour** are nearby shopping destinations with fewer possibilities, but interesting nonetheless. Some shoppers may even want to concentrate on the detours.

At the end of each regional section is a line-up of **Shorter Trips,** good for when time may be limited or when you don't want to be particularly ambitious.

All information in this book is current as of our publication date. Please keep in mind that retail businesses can change names or close without warning because of financial problems, lost leases, owner illness, or a myriad of other reasons. If you come across such a situation or want to update any information in the book, please write to us at:

Golden Sun Books
Box 715
Princeton Junction, NJ
08550

NORTHERN
NEW JERSEY

FORT LEE

Fort Lee sits atop the 400-foot cliffs of the Palisades, its magnificent backdrop moderated somewhat by the fact that it is in the shadow of the George Washington Bridge. The community is a pleasant one nonetheless, an amalgam of high-rise apartment buildings, intimate neighborhoods of modest homes, sophisticated shops, and restaurants that have to be good because they compete with those across the Hudson.

In November 1776, American troops struggled with the British at the fort atop these cliffs before retreating to Valley Forge. Today, these cliffs are also home to a large community of Chinese, Koreans, and Japanese. Many stores in Fort Lee have new owners from Asia, and signs on nearly all shops proclaim that Asian languages are spoken within. Because Asian customers are usually stylish and brand-conscious, the shops of Fort Lee have cultivated a chicness that makes browsing and buying there a delight.

Directions: *From the New Jersey Turnpike and Interstate 80,* follow signs to the local lanes of Interstate 95. Avoid getting in the lanes to the George Washington Bridge. Take the exit for Fort Lee, go toward the river a few blocks, and turn right on Lemoine Avenue (Route 67). The shopping district begins at Main Street, the very first cross street.

Strategies: Park in the Lemoine Avenue-Main Street area, either on the street or in the big municipal lot behind the stores. When you have finished shopping, take Lemoine Avenue south one mile (it becomes Palisade Avenue) to Route 5. Turn left on Route 5 to Edgewater and head south on River Road. On the return, stay north on River Road, threading your way under the George Washington Bridge. Take a left on Myrtle, and at the traffic light at Lemoine Avenue, go left. The stores we list on Lemoine Avenue are in the first shopping center on your right.

Want time out from shopping? The serenity of Fort Lee Historical Park on Hudson Terrace (a road running parallel to Lemoine Avenue but closer to the Palisades) can be restorative. There are leafy walks, benches, a re-created Revolutionary War-era military camp, and a small museum.

 **BEST SHOPPING**

Alpine Designs II. 1637 Palisade Avenue. (201)944-0400. A gift and home furnishings shop with Italian ceramics, Cartier Le Must accessories, and serving pieces in modern and classic designs.

Mary Chancis. 168 Main Street. (201)947-1650. One of the most stylish in-town stores for women, it carries expensive ladies' wear from Italy, France, and England in sizes 2 to 16. However, more of the fashions are in the smaller sizes. Some of the designers include Les Copains, Iceberg, Moschino, Genny, and Blumarine. Cocktail suits are a specialty.

Patchi. 200 Main Street. (201)585-0505. A unique French chocolatier with breathtakingly beautiful trays, silver-look bowls, and baskets that can be filled for wedding and Bar Mitzvah favors. Something from Patchi would make an exquisite corporate gift.

Palisade Jewelers. 249 Main Street. (201)461-4666. This fabulous jewelry and watch store has just had a facelift. Shop for new and pre-owned watches from Rolex, Cartier, Piaget, Patek Philippe, and Tag Heuer. Prices are strongly discounted. They also carry stunning earrings, bracelets, and necklaces with precious and semi-precious stones.

King Frederick's Designer Handbags. 302 Main Street. (201)461-0809. Leather bags from European designers such as Fendi, Moschino, and Versace. Also, small leather goods, costume jewelry, scarves, and accessories. If you don't see what you want, the owners will try to get it for you.

Metropolitan Plant and Flower Exchange. 459 Main Street. (201)944-1050. Flower and plant mavens will adore this large shop packed with fresh and dried blooms, ficus trees, and cacti, and the containers to put them in. Here is where to find those massive stoneware pots from the Orient to put around the pool.

Giorgio Shoes for Women. 2151 Lemoine Avenue. (201)585-9284. Another location, for men's shoes, is at 200 Main Street. (201)585-2411. This elegant bootery for women is in a small shopping center north of the George Washington Bridge. It carries one of the best selections of imported shoes in New Jersey, including cutting-edge designs in flats and heels by Robert Clergerie and Henry Beguelin. The shop also showcases shoes from Via Spiga and Espace, Clergerie's more affordable line. The men's store has high-styled, but comfortable, Italian imports. Merchandise in both stores is quite expensive, but there are sales in late June and January.

Pillow Parlor Inc. 2151 Lemoine Avenue. (201)585-0919. One-of-a-kind pillows are the rage here, as well as contemporary ceramics and accents for the home.

Vogue'M Inc. 2151 Lemoine Avenue. (201)585-9365. This boutique caters to young and stylish women. They carry skinny little dresses, miniskirts, and sleek jeans, most of them imported from Europe. Prices are on the high side.

 **EATS and TASTY TAKEOUT**

The Big Red Tomato. 1205 Anderson Avenue. (201)224-6500. All summer and long into the colder months, fresh beefsteak tomatoes from the owners' father's garden grace the salads, pastas, and pizzas that have made this restaurant a local lunch and dinner favorite. The mozzarella is homemade and the garlic knots, pizza dough seasoned with basil, oregano, and parmesan, are delicious.

Hiram's Roadstand. 1345 Palisade Avenue. **(201)592-9602.** This spot is practically an institution in Fort Lee, where hot dogs, burgers, french fries, and shakes enliven the all-American menu. **Callahan's** is a rival neighbor serving similar fare.

Ruth's Gourmet. 210 Main Street. **(201)461-3904.** Owners Ruth and Harry Artinian make New Jersey's most delicious Middle East specialties in their tiny take-out shop, including their falafel sandwich, hummus, and baba ghanoush. Armenian delicacies abound, plus chicken-to-go, marinated in 11 spices, and cold salads of lentils, cracked wheat, and other grains. Ask and they'll let you try anything in the shop.

 ## WORTH a DETOUR

EDGEWATER

Directions: From Lemoine Avenue in Fort Lee (Route 67), head south 1 mile to Route 5. Turn left on Route 5 (toward Hudson River) and snake down roadway a short distance until you hit traffic light at River Road (Route 505). Go south on River Road.

Gitobet. 726 River Road. **(201)941-7949.** Women from the New Jersey suburbs, New York City, and Rockland County come to Gitobet for their fanciest outfits. Luscious silk, satin, and organza dresses in many different styles. They'll have it made up for you, too.

Yaohan USA. 595 River Road (past the ferryboat Binghamton). **(201)941-9113.** A huge supermarket teeming with foods imported from

Japan and elsewhere in the Orient. Whole families come shopping and murmur their approval when they see foods from home that are impossible to find elsewhere in the metropolitan area. Fresh greens, vegetables, sushi, baked goods, and a variety of canned and packaged delicacies to boggle the mind.

 ## EATS and TASTY TAKEOUT

Beijing Duck House. 880 River Road. (201)945-8825. The specialty of China's capital city, crispy duck, with its crunchy scallions, crepe-like pancakes, and slathering of hoisin sauce, is made to perfection here. And it's always on the menu.

La Vecchia Napoli. 2 Hilliard Avenue (at River Road). (201)941-6799. Overlooking the Hudson, this small Italian restaurant with its starched white tablecloths, lace curtains, and succulent food attracts a crowd from nearby corporations. No Monday lunch.

HOBOKEN

A turn-of-the-century city on the Hudson River, Hoboken is one of New Jersey's gems. Magnificent brownstones line narrow streets, Italian salumerias sit side by side with contemporary coffee bars, and Manhattan seems so close, one could reach right out and touch it. Hoboken is a young city. Scared off by Manhattan rents, men and women fresh out of college discovered they could live cheaply in Hoboken and commute to Wall Street by the PATH. It seems like every shop and eatery in this city, the birthplace of both baseball and Frank Sinatra, is geared toward a young crowd. Dress down appropriately! And make sure you spend a few minutes down at the waterfront in the old Erie Lackawanna Terminal. It is one of the most magnificent buildings in New Jersey.

Directions: *From the New Jersey Turnpike,* take Exit 14-C/Holland Tunnel. Or take Routes 1-9 north into Jersey City. From either approach, get in the left lane as you head down the ramp to the first traffic signal. At the signal, make a left turn onto Hoboken Avenue. Stay on Hoboken Avenue a few blocks. Bear right under the overpass onto Observer Highway. Go almost to the Hudson River. Take a left on Bloomfield Street or Washington Street to be in the heart of Hoboken's action.

From North Jersey, use the New Jersey Turnpike and get off at the Lincoln Tunnel/Exit 17. Bear right at the Hoboken turnoff. Continue through the first traffic light to the bottom of the ramp. Make a right on Park Avenue, then turn left on 14th Street. Go three blocks to Washington Street and turn right. Most good shops start at about 11th Street and go down to First Street.

Strategies: Narrow streets make parking difficult, especially on weekends when the young population of Hoboken is running those important errands that cannot be done during the week. There are meters on Washington Street. Around the Erie Lackawanna Terminal and close by the stores are big parking lots where you can leave your car for the whole day for $8.

 **BEST SHOPPING**

Battaglia's. 319 Washington Street. (201)798-1122. A charming home furnishings shop that carries both the practical (trivets and teapots) and the indulgent (aromatherapy candles and gourmet foods). Because it focuses on the "urban home," Battaglia's has pots, pans, and other cooking equipment in compact sizes.

Erie Street Antiques. 533 Washington Street. (201)656-3596. Beautiful collection of furniture, from French provincial chairs upholstered in leopard to Welsh pine cupboards. But the emphasis is on American Victoriana and the array of sofas from this period is quite impressive.

House Wear. 628 Washington Street. (201)659-6009. If you were setting up your first apartment, you'd find both the frills and the nuts and bolts at this eclectic home furnishings shop owned by Mary and Joe Campagna. Lots of '40s kitchen stuff, attractive china, jelly glass barware, candles, children's books, and gifts.

Anastasia's Accessories. 1006 Washington Street. (201)792-7330. Because it's the '90s, this is an accessories boutique where he and she can browse together. Jewelry, especially the bridal jewelry, silk scarves, handsome ties, small leather goods, and Kenneth Cole handbags. Very nice sales help.

Slumber Party. 904 Bloomfield Street. (201)659-0308. Artist Doug Lindsay has a line of custom-dyed, original fabrics for the home and gifts. Sheets, pillowcases, duvet covers, baby blanket and sheet sets, and patchwork quilts. All colors and combinations to match a room's decor.

Stephane Lesaint Haute Couture. 150 Newark Street. (201)792-0208. One-of-a-kind bridal gowns, dresses for attendants, and formal wear. Open weekday evenings only and Saturday.

 EATS and TASTY TAKEOUT

Texas Arizona. 76 River Street. (201)420-0304. American food, bistro style, located in the downtown district near the PATH Terminal.

Hoboken Farmboy. 229 Washington Street. (201)656-0581. A natural foods market and organic deli that caters to this town's healthy-eating young crowd. The produce is lovely and the bulk grains, nuts, and dried fruits are very fresh.

Small Burgers. 518 Washington Street. **(201)656-7222.** Adorable decor, with cow-patterned booths and lots of '50s diner artifacts.

Benny Tudino's. 622 Washington Street. **(201)792-4132.** Home of the biggest slice of pizza in New Jersey. And it's good, too. Also pastas, eggplant parmegiana subs, and other Italian fast food.

LAFAYETTE

One of the most delightful shopping experiences in New Jersey is off the beaten path in Sussex County where New Jersey really begins to look like the Garden State. Consider Lafayette a real "find." At Olde Lafayette Village, there are several outlets plus a dozen or so specialty shops. Down the road at Lafayette Mill, a revived grist mill which dates back to the 1850s, there are a handful of really good antique shops including a center with 40 dealers (973)383-0065. Stock is ambitious and prices are affordable. There are also shops that sell hard-to-find furniture restoration supplies and do expert caning and rushing.

Directions: Take I-80 West to Route 15 North to the junction of Routes 15 and 94. Or take Route 206 North to Newton. At the center of town, it will join Route 94 North. Take Route 206-94 North out of Newton, and after passing a shopping strip with malls and fast food restaurants, turn right onto Route 94. Lafayette is about five miles away. To get to the antique shops, bear left on Morris Farm Road (Route 659).

Strategies: Park at Lafayette Mill and do the antique shops there and on Route 15. For those in your party who may not want to shop, there's a rushing creek with a covered bridge and a picnic area in the back. When you come out of the Mill parking lot, go left on Morris Farm Road a few hundred feet to the Route 15 intersection and make a right onto Route 15. Go up the hill about half a mile and you will see the outlets of Olde Lafayette Village on the right. Perhaps the best time to come is fall when the farm markets up and down Route 206 are brimming with apples and pumpkins.

 ## BEST SHOPPING

Lafayette Mill Antiques Center. 12 Morris Farm Road. (973)383-0065. The antiques here are really quality, with 40 dealers showing their wares. Many are on the premises weekends. Notables are ***Sign of the Tymes*** upstairs, with its '50s memorabilia, baseball items, Steiff, and advertising items, and ***Denison Ridge Antiques,*** which is loaded with baskets, quilts, and other Americana. The Mill is open every day except Tuesday and Wednesday.

Bogwater Jim. Lafayette Mill. (973)383-6057. A great selection of furniture, china, and what the proprietor calls "maritime artifacts."

Sweet P.E.A.S. Lafayette Mill. (973)579-6338. Owner Patti Bruterri has tastefully blended antiques with gift items and dried flowers. The antique furniture consists largely of wicker and painted bureaus, which would look good in a young girl's room or sunporch. Some pairs of fluted columns in wood, wonderful baskets, and English china.

Silver Willow Inc. Route 15. (973)383-5560. In an old stone house just a few steps from the Mill, this shop blends new and old. Dried flowers, woven throws, and native American items sit side by side with glass and china in showcases. Check out the second floor.

Harriet Hartmann. Corner of Route 15 and Morris Farm Road (in the lower level of Silver Willow). (973)300-0099. Country furniture and accessories, with copper and brass accents.

Cona's Antiques. Morris Farm Road. (973)383-0066. Across the street from Lafayette Mill. Two floors packed with antiques and collectibles. Buffs will enjoy the collection of vintage lunchboxes from the '40s, '50s, and '60s.

Olde Lafayette Village. Route 15 (at the junction of Route 94). (973)383-8323. Some of the national brand outlets include **Bass** for shoes, handbags, and duffle bags and **Izod, Bugle Boy**, and **Van Heusen** for clothing. There are two dozen specialty shops that cover the gamut from candles to kid stuff. **The Garment Center** carries upscale women's clothing such as suits by Kasper and dresses by Jessica Howard. Also wool gabardine slacks and blazers. **Capacity** is an outlet where the clothes are casual and there is a lot of denim. A good place for teenwear. Dexter and Rockport are some of the brands available at **The Shoe Store.**

 EATS and TASTY TAKEOUT

Lafayette General Store Cafe. 12 Morris Farm Road. (973)383-1611. Open for breakfast and lunch, this former general store dating back to 1870 offers overstuffed sandwiches on homemade breads, soups, and homemade baked goods. Sit on picnic tables inside or enjoy a lunch outside.

Lafayette House Restaurant. Olde Lafayette Village. (973)579-3100. A more formal place to have lunch. Well decorated.

 **WORTH a DETOUR**

ANDOVER

Directions: From Lafayette, head south on Route 206 about 12 miles.

In this small village you will find about six antique shops and a large group shop. Check out **Andover Antiques. 118 Route 206, (973)786-5007.** Huge selection of '50s, art deco, sporting collectibles, vintage clothing, furniture, and paintings.

BYRAM

Directions: From Andover, head further south on Route 206.

Lockwood Farms Garden Center. Route 206. (973)347-3010. At the first sign of spring, the garden center brings out an extensive display of both terra cotta and white concrete planters. Some unusual designs, including ones rarely seen. Also annuals and perennials.

The **MALL** at **SHORT HILLS** and **MILLBURN**

With its recent expansion and opening of a parking deck for hundreds of additional cars, The Mall at Short Hills is New Jersey's finest luxury shopping destination. If your feet hold out, you can do Neiman Marcus, Saks Fifth Avenue, Bloomingdale's, Macy's, and Nordstrom's plus shops like Tiffany & Co. and Bottega Veneta. Nearby is the small village of Millburn with its excellent restaurants and unique stores that one would never find in a mall setting.

Directions: Millburn and The Mall at Short Hills are located off Route 24, which runs between Morristown and I-78.

To The Mall at Short Hills from the north, take I-80 West to Route 287 South to Route 24 South and get off at the exit that says Mall/JFK Parkway/Livingston. Circle back under the highway to the mall entrance.

From the New Jersey Turnpike get off at Exit 14, go west on I-78 (local lanes) to Route 24 North and get off at the JFK Parkway/Livingston/Caldwell exit. The mall entrance is the first road on the right.

To Millburn From The Mall, head toward Livingston on the JFK Parkway and turn right on Parsonage Hill Road. Take Parsonage Hill Road past two traffic lights to a stop sign at Old Short Hills Road. Turn right and go downhill past the junior high into the village. You will be on Main Street.

From I-78 get off at the Vauxhall Road-Millburn exit and stay straight on Vauxhall Road past the small strip shopping center on right with the Drug Fair (Millburn Mall). Turn left onto Millburn Avenue and go about a half mile into the village.

Strategies: At The Mall, park in the middle deck. That way, you are equidistant from the mall's bookend anchor stores, Bloomingdale's and Neiman Marcus. If you want to be indulgent, use valet parking at the front of both Saks and Neiman Marcus. The cost is $4 per hour.

In Millburn, park at a meter along Millburn Avenue in the vicinity of the movie theater or swing into the municipal lot on Essex Street near the corner of Main Street.

BEST SHOPPING
The MALL at SHORT HILLS

Aveda. Upper Level. (973)467-4500. Cosmetics and hair preparations made from vegetable sources. Everything is natural and smells heavenly. These products are among the finest on the market.

Black Hound New York. Upper Level. (973)467-2800. The ultimate holiday or hostess gifts are the miniature butter cookies at Black Hound confectionery, ensconced in a bleached Shaker box and tied with black ribbon. The chocolate truffles are heavenly and so are the cakes, although they are rich and costly. Everything is made in the Black Hound's New York bakery. Only Belgian chocolate is used in Black Hound's confections. The almond petals, honeyed slivers of crisply toasted almonds, are addictive.

Bottega Veneta. Upper Level. (973)258-0101. Irresistible leathers. Woven and coated handbags, many in large sizes for women who have a lot to carry around. There are also shoes, sunglasses, wallets. For a small store, it is well stocked.

Crate & Barrel. Upper Level. (973)379-9700. This store goes on and on. Packed with attractive, well-priced home furnishings, china, glassware, furniture, vases, lamps, and you name it. College students and newlyweds can stock up here.

Crouch & Fitzgerald. Upper Level. (973)379-7977. A refined luggage store with the finest bags, carry-ons, briefcases, purses, and wallets. All the best brands are carried, such as Hartmann. There are some unique pieces, including delightful English woven luggage that might not be suitable for air travel but would look smashing if you were driving to a chic bed and breakfast for the weekend. Look for their sales.

Eileen Fisher. Upper Level. (973)376-5111. For women who like comfortable clothes with elastic waists, the whole Fisher line is carried here. Put together a jacket, skirt, and top.

Filofax. Upper Level. (973)258-9773. So you want to get organized. There's no better way to do it than with a Filofax system from England. Many different types of leather-bound calendars, wallets, and address books in rich jewel tones. There's a $35 vinyl organizer perfect for a graduation gift. Prices go up from there. Lizard or croc can be several hundred dollars.

Joan & David. Upper Level. (973)379-2287. Mostly shoes in the supple leathers and beautiful designs that this company is known for. Plus lots of bags in faux croc and sportswear imported from Italy. They carry the whole Joan & David line.

Maraolo. Upper Level. (973)564-5040. Italian shoes for women and men, plus the most darling shoes and sandals for children. Very well designed. And the prices are good. Their ladies' evening shoes from Armani are fabulous.

The Oilily Store. Upper Level. (973)258-0949. Ice cream colors and wild patterns in kids' clothes, with a few adult offerings scattered in. Made in Holland, the Oilily line (pronounced "Oll-ee") is known for its winter coats. For a girl, a warm, oversized Oilily coat might be expensive but it could last three or four seasons and never go out of fashion.

The Wolford Boutique. Upper Level. (973)379-3666. Undergarment chic. Unusual pantyhose, stockings, tights, and leotards imported from Europe, many in wool, silk, and other natural fibers. Expensive, but they wear well. Luscious colors.

French Corner Soho. Lower Level. (973)258-1928. One of the newest stores in the mall, this shop caters to young women, in college and out in the working world, who like well-made, elegant clothes at prices that won't break their pocketbooks. Attractive suits.

Judith Ripka. Lower Level. (973)376-3033. The first New Jersey outpost of a fine Madison Avenue jewelry store, this shop carries spectacular designs in platinum or 18 karat gold with regular or matte finish. Venetian glass and hand-carved intaglios are often used as design elements. Bring in your old pearls and they'll design a necklace "system" that enables the wearer to get a whole day-into-evening jewelry wardrobe out of one piece. Very clever.

Orvis. Lower Level. (973)376-4828. For the fishing enthusiast in your life, this shop carries a range of outdoorsy clothing and accessories. Here's where to find those multi-pocketed vests! But not limited to dressing "on the fly." Lots of looks for dress-down work days, too.

Polo Ralph Lauren. Lower Level. (973)467-4680. Richly appointed salon for displaying everything from tee shirts and shoes to men's and women's high-fashion suits. The Ralph Lauren jewelry is tasteful and nicely priced.

Tiffany & Co. Lower Level. (973)467-3600. It's not the Fifth Avenue store, but it does have a wide range of jewelry, from pens and pins to rings worth thousands of dollars. The store stocks the fine china, glassware, and gifts that Tiffany is noted for the world over. You'd be surprised how reasonable some of their gifts are.

The Walking Co. Lower Level. (973)258-9789. An unusual store that carries shoes and accessories for the sport of walking. Incredible sandals from Denmark, the United States, and England. If you're a walker and never have had on a pair of Mephisto shoes from France, you are missing something. Many people claim these leather and cushioned-sole walkers are the most comfortable on the market today. The only problem is they are in the $240 range. The store carries Mephisto's dress shoes as well.

EATS and TASTY TAKEOUT

Dean & DeLuca. Lower Level. (973)258-1500. Always a host of gourmet sandwiches on hand plus cappuccino, iced drinks, and incredible baked goods.

Joe's American Bar & Grill. Lower Level. **(973)379-4444.** Burgers, excellent sandwiches, salads, and more.

Paparazzi. Lower Level. **(973)467-5544.** Wood-oven baked pizzas and delicious salads make this an excellent spot for lunch or dinner.

NM Cafe. Third Level of Neiman Marcus. **(973)912-0080.** All the choices for the day are set out on a granite counter amid topiaries and flowers.

 ## BEST SHOPPING
MILLBURN

The Paper Pedlar. 681 Morris Turnpike. **(973)376-3385.** Very nice selection of paper plates and party stuff, but the real treasure is in the back. Wholesale prices on super high quality, heavy wrapping paper. It comes in rolls of 5, 12, or 25 feet. Solid colors in high gloss, from white, red, and green for Christmas to deep black and gorgeous maroon for sophisticated wrapping. Many whimsical children's patterns and elegant prints.

Bed Bath & Beyond. 715 Morris Turnpike. **(973)379-4203.** It's hard to resist this home accessories superstore. Well stocked on picture frames, kitchen gadgets, small home appliances, sheets, towels, pillows, and bathroom rugs. An important visit for the college-bound.

Portico Bed and Bath. 752 Morris Turnpike. **(973)564-9393.** Up-to-the-minute furniture and home accessories. Even stunning bunk beds for the kids. Look for the bed linens by Nancy Koltes, N.C. Souther, Anichini, and the vintage goods of Lucille & Henry. Beautiful bath products, gifts, and candles.

S. Marsh. 265 Millburn Avenue. (973)376-7100. For years, Marsh has been reason enough to make the trek to Millburn. A jewelry, silver, and gift shop since 1908, Marsh is the place where brides register their china, crystal, and flatware, and spouses come to pick out distinctive jewelry for important occasions. The selection of fine watches is enormous. Marsh also carries lower-priced jewelry good for graduation and Bat Mitzvah gifts.

U Brew Inc. 319½ Millburn Avenue. (973)376-0973. Stores like this for supplies used in wine and beer making at home are popping up all over the place. A nice selection in all price ranges.

Shala. 343 Millburn Avenue (in the Courtyard). (973)467-7855. This special shop sells painted shelves, stools, and furniture as well as gifts.

Deborah Gilbert Smith. 351 Millburn Avenue. (973)379-7900. Deborah got to know what her clientele wanted when she worked for a large department store. Now she's in her own place, where fashionable women sift through racks of beautiful suits and fancy evening wear.

Designer Jewelry Outlet. 353 Millburn Avenue. (973)467-8899. Brides like to come here for affordable jewelry to wear on the big day. Mostly done with pearls. But there's a lot of other costume jewelry at super prices and jeweled bags for the evening.

Allure. 356 Millburn Avenue. (973)467-8900. Larger women, rejoice. Here's a store that carries very elegant evening clothes of the highest quality, conservative suits for work, and imported French and Italian sports clothes. Sales personnel will keep trying until you are happy.

Kids Decor. 358 Millburn Avenue. (973)379-0095. Everything for a kid's room, from beds and nightstands to desks and chairs. Clean, modern lines and lots of fun stuff. A child who got to pick out a room here would be very lucky, indeed.

Bear-a-dise. 359 Millburn Avenue. (973)376-2405. Literally thousands of stuffed bears, all dressed differently, just waiting to be "adopted." They'll send a bear anywhere.

Ultima Moda. 382 Millburn Avenue. (973)376-4770. Men's suits, jackets, shorts, and ties imported from Italy. High fashion for the sleek of physique.

Gotham City Clothing Company. 391 Millburn Avenue. (973)467-9797. Just settled in new, larger quarters, Gotham has been the "in" store for New Jersey teenagers for a decade. Gail, the savvy owner, knows what young girls like and what their mothers like to spend. The store carries the creations of designers like Betsey Johnson and Cynthia Rowley plus new and used jeans, cotton tops, sweaters, skirts, and floaty prom dresses. The sales help is understanding and fun!

Beverlee Fisher Design. 508 Millburn Avenue. (973)467-4477. The shop's designs with silk and other artificial flowers are simply breathtaking. Centerpieces, front hall arrangements, and party decor. No one would know these aren't the real thing.

DWI. 517 Millburn Avenue. (973)379-4001. The store is as fantastic as its windows. Young, kicky clothing that follows the current trends. Teenagers will love it.

Nita Ideas. 518 Millburn Avenue. (973)379-7711. Another contemporary clothing store for teens and women plus some adorable children's things. Build a wardrobe without breaking the bank.

Priscilla of Boston. 565 Millburn Avenue. (973)376-2345. Don't be put off by the fact that you have to be buzzed in. This is the store for brides, their gowns, headpieces, and accessories. Also beautiful dresses for attendants.

Forgotten Times. 27 Main Street. (973)376-4148. Exquisite antiques, many of them in the

Chinese and English porcelain line. Also beautiful gifts and scents. A very large store.

The Backrub Shoppe. 41 Main Street. (973)912-9802. On Main heading north you will find one of Millburn's most unusual shops. In addition to the balms and exercise equipment for those with back pain, this store is in the business of giving backrubs. Create an oasis of calm in the middle of a hectic day with a stress-reducing backrub. The concept started in California, but now it is in full bloom in New Jersey. This shop has another outpost in Upper Montclair.

George Remolina Designs. 55 Main Street. (973)467-1007. South of Millburn Avenue, this small shop sells and restores antique jewelry. An exquisite selection. Anyone would cherish a gift from this shop.

 ## EATS and TASTY TAKEOUT

Cafe Main. 40 Main Street. (973)467-2222. Here the fare is contemporary American. Order a burger – made of beef, turkey, or veggies. On the menu are pastas and caesar salad with grilled chicken or shrimp.

J.P. Lee's Mongolian Barbecue. 318 Millburn Avenue. (973)912-9899. You know the routine. Heap a little of this and a little of that on your plate, pour on the sauce, and let it cook on the kettle stove. They also serve a great lunch buffet.

Millburn Delicatessen. 328 Millburn Avenue. (973)379-5800. Order your sandwich at the counter and sit down to dine. The Sloppy Joe is the house specialty, a triple decker on rye with roast beef, turkey, cole slaw, and Russian dressing. You can have it with other fillings as well.

Syd's Hot Dogs. 2933 Vauxhall Road (in the Millburn Mall). (908)686-2233. Syd's hot dogs are known throughout the state. Have them grilled or steamed, with sauerkraut or without. Take them home, too. The place also serves a good corned beef sandwich for $3.95.

MONTCLAIR and UPPER MONTCLAIR

Judging from the estates along Mountain Avenue, Montclair is a moneyed town and the shops reflect it. And yet there is a funky side to this yuppified community. Off Bloomfield Avenue, Church Street has been revitalized. Kicky new stores sell contemporary apparel, children's clothing and room decor, stationery, and antiques. Montclair contains many fine restaurants and its cinemas show first-run films that don't seem to come to other movie theaters in New Jersey. Upper Montclair shopping, while still fun, is older money. The shops are elegant and not as daring as their counterparts down the mountain.

Directions: *To Montclair from the Garden State Parkway,* exit at Bloomfield Avenue and head north. After one mile, you will come into the main shopping district of Montclair. All the side shopping streets come off Bloomfield Avenue.

From Interstate 80, take Route 23 South (Pompton Avenue). In Verona, Pompton Avenue hits Bloomfield Avenue. Turn left to Montclair.

To Upper Montclair from Montclair, head north on Bloomfield Avenue, then turn right on Valley Road, and follow that 1 1/2 miles to the village center.

Strategies: Try to park around Church Street, North Fullerton Street, or the Crescent Municipal Lot and walk around Montclair. Then get in the car and drive to Upper Montclair. The best parking is in the metered lot opposite the railroad station behind the stores on Valley Road. If you have time, visit the little-known but pleasing Montclair Art Museum at 3 South Mountain

Avenue. (973)746-5555. Montclair was an artists' colony in the mid-19th century and many of the artists who lived in town are represented here.

BEST SHOPPING
MONTCLAIR

Semplice. 430 Bloomfield Avenue. (973)783-1950. A trend-setting home furnishings store that looks like it belongs in Soho. New sofas, chairs, and decorative and occasional pieces, but with a retro look. The store carries the most exciting lighting around.

So Unusual. 571 Bloomfield Avenue (at Maple Plaza). (973)783-7442. Vintage clothing, specializing in the '50s. Dozens of poodle skirts. Also costume jewelry, Bakelite, pop beads. Great place to outfit yourself for a party.

Lion Gate Interiors. 19 Church Street. (973)783-4611. If you are a fan of Italian tableware like Deruta, you won't be disappointed. This shop has a large stock of this practical and lovely china from Northern Italy. The interior design section of the store specializes in custom furniture and English fabrics and wallpaper such as Lee Jofa, Sanderson, Osborne & Little, and Colefax & Fowler, all 10 to 15 percent off. The design staff is very helpful and very professional.

American Sampler/Dobbs Ltd. 20-26 Church Street. (973)744-1474. Two stores side by side sharing one owner, where the decorative arts are prized beyond all others. Candles, women's casual cotton and linen clothing (they carry the Flax line, including new plus sizes), hats, and scents at Dobbs. Antiques, contemporary folk art, superb silver jewelry, and upholstered furniture next door.

Dexterity. 30 Church Street. (973)746-5370. One of the best craft galleries in the state, Dexterity is certainly a visual feast. Wonderful pottery, stunning glass, and kaleidoscopes.

Martin Williams Antiques and Home Decor.
41 Church Street. (973)744-1149. New and old
items mesh in this spacious shop. The shop's
armoires and corner cabinets are the best. Some
baskets, some Adirondackiana.

**Neo Mosaics. 43-A Church Street. (973)509-
0600.** Open Wednesdays through Saturdays
from noon to 5 p.m., this working studio-shop
offers vases, mirrors, and other small pieces of
furniture created through the process of "pique
assiette," in which shards of objects are embed-
ded in plaster to create new art. The mirrors
made with pieces of broken tile, vintage plates,
and stained glass are must haves!

**Barbara's Place. 53 Church Street. (973)655-
1700.** A children's store catering to very young
ladies who are attending very grown-up events
such as weddings, communions, and parties.
Originally in Rutherford, Barbara's Place opened
on Church Street last Christmas and already has
a reputation for carrying the full dress line of Joan
Calabrese, an American manufacturer of the
finest (and priciest) girls' wear. Other manufacturers include Sylvia Whyte, Posie, Pegeen, and
Barbara Canfer. There are white and peach-
colored, beribboned shoes by Posie, straw hats,
gloves, and other accessories. The store also has
clever crib blankets and adorable clothing for
boys and girls in infant and toddler sizes.

Noel's Place. 173 Glenridge Avenue. (973)744-
2156. Chinese, Victorian-era, and art deco
antiques side by side in a terrific shop. (There is a
mini-antique district along Glenridge, with shops
like **Station West** at 225, and **JoElynn Welsh's
Real Paint** at 299.)

Noteworthy. 24 South Fullerton Avenue.
(973)783-1522. A stationer packed with invitations, personal notes, and children's writing paper.
Pick out blank invitations and Noteworthy will
typeset them using the latest computer technol-
ogy. Adds a custom touch to birthday, anniversary, holiday, and shower invitations.

EATS and TASTY TAKEOUT

A Taste of Asia. 706 Bloomfield Avenue (across from Fresh Fields). (973)744-3525. One of the only Malaysian restaurants in New Jersey, Taste of Asia serves a terrific lunch special. Soup, appetizers like pie tee (crisp little cases filled with vegetables), and a main course for $7.95.

The Crescent Cafe. 18 South Fullerton Avenue. (973)509-8886. Set in an enclosed mall a block off Bloomfield Avenue, the Crescent Cafe serves breakfast, excellent sandwiches, and salads. Quiet, nice atmosphere.

 ## BEST SHOPPING

UPPER MONTCLAIR

Chelsea Square. 601 Valley Road. (973)746-6468. As you open the door to this fragrance shop, the sweet smell of lotions and soaps and herb-based skin products hits the olfactory nerve. The owners, Larry and Sandy Kelman, carry hard-to-find Kiehl products, Crabtree & Evelyn, Caswell-Massey, and other scents and potions from Great Britain. The scented shelf-liner paper in great designs smells heavenly.

Tesori. 618 Valley Road. (973)655-1511. Bed linens, table settings, and bath products imported from Italy and France. Fine manufacturers like Anichini and Palais Royale are joined by the best American bedsheet designers like Nancy Koltes. The store carries beautiful tableware, including the pottery designs of New Yorker Barbara Eigen, who is known for her ceramic gourd tureens and stunning pitchers. Catch their fabulous sales in June and after Christmas.

Alex. 620 Valley Road. (973)746-4800. The best women's apparel store in the region. Spectacular suits and dressy clothes. They carry top designers.

Try to visit during a trunk show in spring or fall.

Threadneedle Street. 195 Bellevue Avenue. (973)783-1336. A sweet antique shop with English fabrics for sale. Transferware, English silver, gorgeous pillows, prints, and paintings priced reasonably.

Wit's End Gift Shop. 208 Bellevue Avenue. (973)744-7917. The finest china from England, Portugal, and Italy, including large service pieces. Contemporary art glass, lamps, and fine crafts. It's a treat just to browse here.

 ## EATS and TASTY TAKEOUT

Arturo's Brick Oven Pizza Co. 223 Bellevue Avenue. (973)744-2300. Try this thin-crust, tasty, brick-oven-baked pizza with different toppings, including one with low-fat mozzarella cheese.

 ## WORTH a DETOUR

CALDWELL

Directions: From Montclair, take Bloomfield Avenue north through Verona into Caldwell, a distance of about 2 miles.

What A Racquet. 468 Bloomfield Avenue. (973)228-3066. New Jersey's tennis haven. No matter what your level, this place has a racquet for you. Very nice sales help. Also equipment for other racquet sports.

PASSAIC

Directions: *From Upper Montclair,* take Bellevue Avenue down the mountain to Broad Street. Turn left on Broad Street and follow that out to Route 3. Take Route 3 East toward New York and get off at the Main Avenue exit. Go toward Passaic.

Jan, Jill & Jon. 170 Main Avenue. (973)777-4670. This is a large shop with the finest merchandise, including art deco and art nouveau. The Tiffany lamps and bronzes are magnificent. One of the few antique shops that take credit cards.

MORRISTOWN

General George Washington spent the winter of 1779-80 in Morristown and the vestiges of this city's colonial past are still evident in the layout of the central shopping district, the architecture, and the feel of the distinctly upscale shops. The Green is the center of business and governmental life and the shops and restaurants that crowd the area, such as Epstein's department store and The Gap, are host daily to county workers, lawyers, judges, and business people.

Directions: *From the south,* take Route 287 North to Route 24 Exit/ Morristown. Get on Route 24 West. It becomes South Street, which leads to The Green (the town center).

From I-80, get off on Route 287 South and go to the Lafayette Avenue exit. Stay straight at the first traffic light, crossing Ridgedale Avenue. At the second traffic light at Morris Street, turn right to The Green.

Strategies: Morristown is the county seat, so it is packed with cars. Best to park in municipal lots off South Street or in metered parking nearby to reach shops there and on The Green. There is underground parking at Headquarters Plaza on Speedwell Avenue. Drive to shopping on the town outskirts. You may want to visit the Morristown National Historical Park, where you will find the elegant Ford Mansion, once Washington's headquarters, located at 230 Morris Street, and the visitors' center on Tempe Wick Road at Jockey Hollow. Call (973)539-2085.

 **BEST SHOPPING**

The Teaching Room. 151 South Street. (973)540-8358. Books, toys, materials for learning. Good for teachers and parents who want to go beyond simple play.

American Craft Gallery. 163 South Street. (973)538-6720. An interesting store with pottery, folk-art sculptures, wearing apparel, candles, and other crafts.

Coletree Antiques and Interiors. 166 South Street. (973)993-3011. Really fabulous antiques. Worth a trip in.

The Dain Shoppe. 8 Community Place. (973)539-7586. The kind of women's store that used to be in every town but is rapidly disappearing. Personal fittings on bras. They stock all sizes, especially in minimizers. Exquisite lingerie, some perfect for bridal trousseaus.

Dressed to the Nines. 19 Pine Street. (973)285-9081. You know how hard it is to find a good dress. This is one of the best shops for fancy women's clothing for formal parties, proms, or for the mother of the bride. Very congenial sales help.

Enjou Chocolatiers Inc. 8 DeHart Street. (973)993-9090. Here the chocolates are gourmet and in as many shapes as one can think of. They'll even do custom shapes for companies and wedding favors. Incredible selections at Christmas and Easter. A gift basket from Enjou is the ultimate!

Hop & Vine. 11 DeHart Street. (973)993-3191. Supplies for the home brewing of wine and beer, a growing hobby among New Jerseyans. Very nice and knowledgeable personnel.

Knit One, Purl Too! 43 Park Place. (973)644-9588. Huge selection of yarn, both wool and synthetic, for sweaters, coats, baby items, and more. Shop gives private and group knitting lessons.

Morristown Antiques Center. 45 Market Street (Route 202). (973)734-0900. There are 100 dealers represented here. Some have tiny shelves and others large booths, but everything is of top quality. Decorative items, costume jewelry, small pieces of furniture, clocks, paintings, rugs, and sports items. Open daily.

Garden Off the Green. 54 Bank Street (Route 202 South as it comes off the Green). (973)292-9393. For the prettiest urns, flower pots, and garden ornaments, see this shop's incredible collection. Also garden implements and neat gifts for people who like to garden. The shop has its own parking.

Square Luggage. 19 Washington Street. (973)539-1631. The grand-daddy of luggage stores. Square has everything, including all the latest pull luggage from Lark, Delsey, Samsonite, Travel Pro, and others. Prices are excellent. There are oversized duffels for camp and college, manufacturers' close-outs, and small leather goods. They also do monogramming and quick luggage repairs. Shoppers out for a bargain can buy unclaimed repairs. Square has a branch at 320 Route 10 West in East Hanover next to Daffy's, (973)884-0209.

Del's Novelty Co. 84-86 Elm Street. (973)538-5237. Everything you ever needed for a party, such as paper goods, invitations, hats, gag gifts, and lots of interesting favors. Also costumes, pinatas, balloons. This is the place to come when you need prizes or giveaways for school bazaars and fairs.

The Health Shoppe. 66 Morris Street (in the Midtown Shopping Center). (973)538-9131. A huge selection of health and macrobiotic foods, cosmetics, vitamins, home health remedies, and books on living healthy, as well as a natural foods bakery-deli.

Cigar Cafe. 44 Morris Street. (973)285-5377. Get ready for a trip back to a time when men (and some women) used to linger over a fine cigar at a private club. Not a private club nor a cafe, really, this is a place for cigar smokers to hang out in a convivial atmosphere amidst deep leather chairs and magazines. One can buy cigars and accessories for smoking them. If you've never smoked, the staff can teach you about the connoisseurship of cigars.

Winston's Discount Center. 46 Speedwell Avenue. (973)455-9768. Expectant parents come for the full array of carriages, strolles, and baby items, but it doesn't stop there. Once the baby comes, parents shop for toys and gadgets to aid in the child's development. The shop has been here for years and the prices are excellent.

Richard Bevan Furniture and Antiques. 166 Ridgedale Avenue (just before Domb Lighting). (973)984-3140. Antique and new furniture direct from England and Ireland. Some country pieces, some formal pieces. Stop by often since shipments arrive every few weeks.

Sooo Many Shoes Warehouse. 30 Lafayette Avenue (next to Staples). (973)734-0818. This is a real find. A top-quality discount shoe store where you'll find everything from sneakers and sandals to high-fashion pumps. Designers include Joan & David, Palizzio, Margaret Jerrold, Sesto Meucci, Via Spiga, DKNY, Kenneth Cole, and Robert Clergerie. White silk bridal pumps in varying heel heights can be had at a huge discount. They also stock handbags, clothing, and Berkshire pantyhose. Open every day but Tuesday. Late nights are Wednesday and Thursday.

 EATS and TASTY TAKEOUT

C'est Cheese. 64 South Street. (973)267-2941. A gourmet catering shop that has sandwiches, soups, and excellent salads for takeout. Try the shop's baked goods. This shop may have started out with its main focus on cheese, but now cheese takes a backseat to all the other delectables.

Calaloo Cafe. 190 South Street. (973)993-1100. Innovative fare with a bent toward regionalized American cooking, such as New Orleans and Santa Fe.

Moghul Restaurant. 35 Morris Street. (973)631-1100. Indian fare with flair. Close to The Green. Lunch, to order off menu or to select from the extensive buffet. Not open on Mondays.

Pazzo Pazzo. 74 Speedwell Avenue (across from Headquarters Plaza). (973)898-6606. Upscale Italian restaurant, lovely for lunch, 11:30 a.m. to 2:30 p.m., weekdays only.

 **WORTH a DETOUR**
EAST HANOVER

Directions: *From Morristown,* head north on Route 287 to Route 10 East. Go approximately four miles to East Hanover.

Teen Elegance. 50 Route 10 West (around the back of a strip mall near the intersection of Ridgedale Road). (973)515-8141. It's tough to buy formal clothes for teenagers — they hate what you love and love what you hate. Not so at this store. Teen Elegance carries nicely priced dresses for Bar and Bat Mitzvahs, proms, and formal affairs that both you and your teen will adore. Shoppers often find two or three outfits here. Some nice suits for young women, too. Sales staff is supportive and comforting.

Calico Corners. 310 Route 10 West. (973)887-3905. Decorative fabrics for clothing, draperies, and upholstery at mill close-out prices. Bedspreads and slipcovers can be purchased as well.

Daffy's. 346 Route 10 West. (973)428-0360. Off-price designer clothing for women, men, and children. Many of the women's and men's clothes are imported from France and Italy – you'll see some Lagerfeld, Armani, Ferre, Valentino, and Les Copains. Kids' imports are from France and Italy, but there is also Oshkosh, Ralph Lauren, and Flapdoodles. Children's shoes are super and there are high-quality toys. Excellent buys in men's tuxedos and formal shirts, underwear, sport clothes, and leathers and suedes in season. Lingerie comes from the best designers like Natori. Note: other Daffy's stores are in Elizabeth on Route 1; in Paramus on Route 4 West; in Wayne at the Wayne Towne Shopping Center; and on Paterson Plank Road, North Bergen.

WHIPPANY

Directions: From Morristown, head north on Route 287 to Route 10 East. Go approximately two miles to Whippany.

Fox's Off-Price Ladies Designer Clothing. 184 Route 10 West. (973)884-3634. A branch of a super Long Island discount store, this shop has clothes for work from top designers, some dressy clothes, and lots of fabulous pants and tops. Look for Diesel jeans and Calvin Klein's CK brand.

JR Tobacco World. 301 Route 10 East. (973)687-0800. Practically wholesale prices on cigars, cigarettes, and tobacco accoutrements. Also, perfumes at 70 percent off department store prices and gourmet imported candies. Very busy before Christmas. Has a wine and cigar bar.

PARAMUS

When comedians joke that the town of Paramus was covered over for a shopping mall, there might be a little truth in that jest. From Teaneck to Fair Lawn along Route 4 and from Rochelle Park to Ridgewood along Route 17, there are malls, malls, and more malls. Some are humongous, like the newly enlarged Garden State Plaza, and some are strip centers that harbor four or five stores. No matter, this is a shopper's paradise, and a day is hardly enough to cover everything.

Directions: *From the Garden State Parkway,* take the exit for Route 4 East to Paramus and New York.

From the western extension of the New Jersey Turnpike, get on Interstate 80 West and connect with Route 17 North.

Strategies: Bergen County still has blue laws, which means no Sunday shopping. As a result, Saturdays along Routes 4 and 17 are chaotic. Weekday shopping is much more enjoyable.

 **BEST SHOPPING**

DSW Shoe Warehouse. 60 Route 17 North (directly after the Farview Avenue exit). (201)291-0505. Designer and brand name shoes 20 to 50 percent off.

Rudi's Pottery, Silver & China. 182 Route 17 North. (201)265-6096. This discount store bills itself as a "shopping experience," and it is. Just ensconced in new quarters adjacent to where it was for many years, Rudi's carries fine and every-day china from many manufacturers, including

Lenox, Villeroy & Boch, Wedgwood, and Royal Crown Derby. There are beautiful serving pieces, kitchen equipment, Hummels, Lladro, and flatware from companies like Sasaki, Kirk, Reed & Barton, and International.

Garden State Plaza. Route 17 South or Route 4 East. (201)843-2404. Once just average, this mall has turned into a fantastic shopping arena with the addition of Neiman Marcus, Nordstrom's, Lord & Taylor, and hundreds of smaller shops. Marble and statuary are everywhere. Even the new food court is sensational. For trendy clothing for teenagers and young women, visit **BCBG Max Azria,** (201)368-5722. It is located on the second level between Lord & Taylor and Nordstrom's. On the mall's first level are several other shops that deserve a look. **Impostors,** (201)291-1191, carries copies of Tiffany, Van Cleef & Arpels, Yurman, Lagos, and Cartier jewelry that are very tempting, especially when they look like the real thing. **The Romaye Collection,** (201)291-9334, features knitted suits and separates, lightweight for spring and heavier for winter, which are very attractive and reasonable. Made in Mexico, these garments look like St. John, only without the hefty price tag. Sizes up to 18 or 20. **Shoe-Chic,** (201)291-9373, is where brides can find a pair of contemporary-styled white heels or party-goers can locate a pair of sexy, black satin slingbacks. This shop carries only formal and dyeable shoes from designers such as Stuart Weitzman and Vanessa Noel, plus handbags and accessories. Another store location is in the Mall at IV, 289 Route 4 West.

Holly Sue. 703 Route 17 South. (201)652-1960. This is the place to go for those brides who would like to browse for china, crystal, and silver at discount prices. Place settings of Ceralene, Bernardaud, Rosenthal, Tiffany, Royal Doulton, Lenox, and Portmeirion, among other top brands, are displayed. Discount is about 20 percent. The same discount applies to Baccarat crystal (not all patterns stocked here). The Lalique glass sculptures make fine gifts.

Kalkin & Co. Route 17 and Ridgewood Avenue (at The Fashion Center). (201)670-8068. Almost a museum, Kalkin showcases the finest domestic and imported home accessories in small lighted rooms and nooks. Baccarat, Lalique, fine china, exotic bed linens, bathroom hardware in chrome and brass, lamps, trays, and writing papers. Don't miss the sturdy rubber doormats in hunting, Impressionist art, and nautical motifs, among others. This is the place to visit when you need an impressive gift. Next door, Kalkin-owned **Pinch Penny** carries Kalkin's markdowns and closeouts as well as its own lower-priced but attractive merchandise.

Oh So Dressy. 154 Route 4 East. (201)843-8102. Located next to Loehmann's, this single-concept store has a vast selection of dressy dresses – sequins, lace, satin, sexy, low-cut, and high-necked. They are available in sizes from petite to large. Prom shoppers, take notice. When you don't want to spend a bundle, try this place. Most dresses are around $60 to $100.

Loehmann's and Loehmann's Clearance. 180 Route 4 East (west of Route 17). (201)843-1880. After extensive renovations, Loehmann's is again open and beside it is the new clearance center, which receives merchandise from the main store at the end of each season. So if you need a bathing suit in January and don't have to have the very latest, shop the clearance center. In the main store, those who know labels do best. The Back Room carries the most sought after designer goods and dressy pieces. Note: other Loehmann's are in Florham Park, East Brunswick, Green Brook, and Cherry Hill.

Gap Outlet. Route 4 East and Forest Avenue (in the Bergen Mall). (201)843-1502. When a Gap selling season is over, which may be only a month, odds and ends of well-made clothing usually end up here. You'll also find irregulars from

Banana Republic. Lots of jeans and tops. Big on Baby Gap merchandise, too.

Off 5th. **Route 4 East and Forest Avenue (in the Bergen Mall). (201)291-1949.** This big off-price branch of Saks Fifth Avenue carries past-season designer merchandise and extra stock from Folio, Saks' catalog business. Although these outlets are in Pennsylvania, Massachusetts, and Florida, among other states, this is one of the best. Merchandise may be off-season, but not so far off. Handsome men's and women's Tse cashmere sweaters selling for 30 percent off in regular retailers' January sales were about 70 percent off here. So were Gucci shoes and clothing for women, designer ballgowns from Christian Lacroix (some with original $17,000 price tags), and men's suits and dress shirts from Italy. The deeply discounted sheets and towels were too good to be true.

David's Bridal. **153 Route 4 West. (201)342-8113.** Located in the Caldor Shopping Mall, David's has designer wedding gowns and bridesmaids dresses in stock. Prices are discounted. They also carry bridal accessories such as headpieces, veils, trains, gloves, and petticoats.

Jewelry Exchange at IV. **275 Route 4 West. (201)488-6055.** Thirty-six jewelers in one space, most carrying gold chains and rings of similar design. Prices are discounted and one can bargain. Most jewelers will do repairs.

 EATS and TASTY TAKEOUT

The Fireplace. **718 Route 17 North. (201)444-2362.** Charcoal-grilled cheeseburgers and hot dogs. Also barbecued chicken. Order at the counter, then move to the dining room to load up with pickles, onions, and other condiments.

Jose Tejas. **65 Route 4 West. (201)291-0444.** Located in a small shopping center with parking aplenty, this festive restaurant is one where shoppers can lunch on Mexican specialties.

 **WORTH a DETOUR**

HACKENSACK

Directions: *From Route 4,* take Hackensack Avenue south. It is also known as River Street. Turn right on Passaic Street to Main Street where most of the smaller shops are.

Pan Handlers, Inc. 120 Passaic Street. (201)488-4442. For home or commercial users, this shop discounts paper goods and throwaway serving pieces for parties, chafing frames and covered pans, glassware, china, bulk food, bar supplies, janitorial supplies, and cooking equipment. Spied at Pan Handlers: glasses as low as 50 cents a piece and the biggest plastic salad bowl you ever saw for $15.

Riverside Square Mall. Route 4 West at Hackensack Avenue. (201)489-2212. It is easy to spend the day in this two-level mall anchored by **Saks Fifth Avenue** and **Bloomingdale's**. Because New Yorkers come in droves to take advantage of the fact that New Jersey has no sales tax on clothing, the sophistication level of merchandise in most stores is high. The mall has **Workbench, Pottery Barn,** and other fine chain stores. A favorite shop is the children's wear store *La Petite Gaminerie,* 167 Riverside Square, (201)488-1806. They have the best of France and Italy for the little princess and prince.

Tennis Outlet. 399 River Street. (201)343-3331. The original is on Route 17 in Saddle River, but this downtown store has more space for tennis and golf clothing, racquets, sneakers, and paraphernalia. Prices about 15 percent off retail for all the top brands like Wilson, Prince, and K-Swiss. Pay cash and get a greater reduction. Terrific-looking tennis separates for women, like those by Tail and X 40, are a specialty.

Wicker Warehouse Inc. 195 South River Street. (201)342-6709. More wicker and rattan than Sofas, you've ever seen in one place. loveseats, living room chairs, and dining sets. Some items have no brand name. Or you can pay a little more for Ficks Reed, Lloyd, and Lane. Smaller items such as baskets and bathroom accessories are carried as well.

LODI

Directions: *From Paramus,* take Route 17 North. Get off at the Essex Street exit, turn right.

Milton Decorator Fabrics. **338 Essex Street. (201)843-8899.** If you are looking for highly polished cottons and chintzes for drapery and upholstery, Milton carries Robert Allen, Ralph Lauren, Yang, Mario Buatta for Schumacher, and other designer fabrics at about 40 percent off retail. The store has been redesigned and restocked after the building next door burned and caused smoke and water damage. Be sure to look at Milton's new line of custom furniture. It's gorgeous. Helpful sales people.

Party Box. Route 17 South. (201)843-3712. Discount prices on paper plates, cups, plastic utensils, and other catering supplies. Personalized balloons and cocktail napkins are done on short notice.

RIVER EDGE

Directions: *From the Garden State Parkway,* get off at Route 17 North. Just past Syms you will see the turnoff to Midland Park/River Edge. Take this road three miles to its T-intersection with Kinderkamack Road.

Heading west on Route 4, after Riverside Square Mall turn right past the first group of stores where it says "Kinderkamack Road-Bergenfield." Take that north into River Edge.

WOB Lingerie. **920 Kinderkamack Road. (201)265-6116.** The initials stand for Wizard of Bras and is this title ever deserved! Thousands of bras, 20 percent off retail prices, from manufacturers of top imports such as Wacoal and Hanro plus domestics such as Lily and Bali. Strapless, backless, convertible, minimizer, and nursing bras in sizes to 48 DDD. Rarely does one find discounted the lush cotton underwear from Hanro and Natori, together with Calvin Klein and Jockey briefs, and Olga tummy-slimming underwear. Donna Karan workout wear, CK socks, and Vanity Fair nightgowns are also featured. When you arrive, park in the rear.

TEANECK

Directions: *Heading east on Route 4* from Paramus, take the Webster Avenue exit and turn right. Make a right on Alfred Avenue.

Lew Magram Ltd. Outlets. 414 Alfred Avenue (at the end of the street). (201) 833-8179. Discontinued and past-season items from the Lew Magram Ltd. catalog of fine women's clothing. About 50 to 70 percent off catalog prices.

RIDGEWOOD

Minutes from the malls and highways of Paramus, Ridgewood is a quiet town of large homes, parks, and upscale shops. The commercial core of the village leads from the railroad station down East Ridgewood Avenue, filling the side streets with apparel and home furnishing stores, gourmet takeout food shops, restaurants, coffee bars, and service businesses. Close your eyes and you could be in Greenwich, Connecticut; Scarsdale, New York; Newton, Massachusetts; or any one of a number of affluent East Coast villages.

Directions: *From Route 17 North,* take the

Ridgewood Avenue, Ridgewood exit and go about one mile into town.

From Route 287 North, take Route 208 South to the Goffle Road-Ridgewood/Midland Park exit. Circle down onto Goffle Road and continue straight two miles to a traffic light at Godwin Avenue. Turn right onto Godwin and Ridgewood center will be one mile down the road. Follow Godwin Avenue around to the left, pass under the railroad tracks, and make a right onto Broad Street. This is the heart of the shopping area.

 **BEST SHOPPING**

Persnickety. 9 East Ridgewood Avenue. (201)447-8841. A delightful decorating shop that mixes upholstered pieces, fabrics, lamps, dried flowers, frames, and other home accessories. Although the shop carries high-end fabrics from Colefax & Fowler and Osborne & Little, it always showcases some great-looking fabrics in the mid-ranges for reupholstering that old den couch.

Sweet Feet Ltd. 41 East Ridgewood Avenue. (201)447-5433. Look in the windows for trendy shoes for women and teens at reasonable prices. They carry Sam & Libby and Kaminski straw hats and bags.

Montana Inc. 57 East Ridgewood Avenue. (201)652-4321. Ridgewood's trendiest store for men, women, and kids. It features Italian and some French and English imports like Replay and Sons, Diesel, Iceberg. The jeans are fabulous.

Duxiana. 63 East Ridgewood Avenue. (201)670-4488. If you want a specially made bed that supports your spine, you can find it in this store, a branch of a Manhattan bedding shop. But Duxiana also carries down comforters, terrific-looking sheets and duvets, and a broad range of pillows, both for sleep and decorative purposes.

Biondina. 67 East Ridgewood Avenue.

(201)444-3732. Beautiful, easy-to-wear clothing from Tapp and other manufacturers. Also bathing suits, lingerie, stunning shoes, handbags, and unusual belts from Judith Jack.

Laura Ashley Home. 171 East Ridgewood Avenue. **(201)670-0868.** Here you will find soft cushioned furniture in all the Laura Ashley ice cream colors, plus lamps, bedding, and tableware to match. They also stock a wide range of Ashley fabrics, including ones suitable for decorating children's rooms.

Victoria's. 189 East Ridgewood Avenue. **(201)612-1116.** A huge selection of delightful children's clothes awaits parents, grandparents, and gift givers. Look for the tiny Lilly Pulitzer dresses and playsuits. Angelic white dresses for parties, weddings, and religious occasions as well as rough and tumble wear for little boys.

Fox's Off Price Ladies Designer Clothing. 230 East Ridgewood Avenue. **(201)444-1842.** See the Whippany entry under Morristown for a description.

Country Curtains. 15 South Walnut Street. **(201)444-4767.** One of three Country Curtain shops in New Jersey, this large store carries curtains, valences, sheers, and coordinating pillows that look custom made, even though they are right off the rack. Curtains come in many styles and fabrics, from high gloss chintz to casual denim and eyelet. The people who work here couldn't be nicer and more helpful.

Junk. 45 North Broad Street. **(201)444-6464.** Home furnishings shop that, belying its name, has great style. Browse among faux-finished furniture, pottery, aromatherapy candles, a terrific card and wrapping paper section, and other items for the way we live today.

Marilyn of Monroe. 39 Godwin Avenue. **(201)447-3123.** The accent is on vintage clothing, some of it dating back to the Victorian era, Bakelite and old costume jewelry, hats, shoes, and other accessories. Going formal and want to make a statement? The gowns from the '50s are in mint condition. Also a spot for Halloween and theatrical costumes.

 EATS and TASTY TAKEOUT

Blue Moon Mexican Cafe. 23 Chestnut Street. (201)689-0861. Eat your fill of tacos, tortillas, burritos, and salads at this attractively decorated restaurant on one of Ridgewood's side streets.

The Best of Everything. 29 Oak Street. (201)670-7575. Proprietor Lou Torelli has one of the best prepared-foods sections in town. Always on the menu are shrimp and chicken francese, pastas, lasagnas, eggplant dishes, and salads with the freshest ingredients. Try the semolina bread from Hoboken.

Cafe Winberie. 30 Oak Street. (201)444-3700. Winberie's is known for traditional fare, such as soups, salads, burgers, and grilled chicken.

Village Green Cafe. 36 Prospect Street (at the corner of Hudson Street). (201)445-2914. Come to a restaurant/tearoom that is so cozy you might think you are in a friend's dining room. The soups are delicious and sandwiches are served with a scrumptious caesar salad. Try the salad sampler with curried chicken, Tuscany shrimp, couscous, and tabouli.

 **WORTH a DETOUR**

MIDLAND PARK

Directions: *From Ridgewood,* go north on Glen Avenue. Stores are mixed into a residential neighborhood.

From Route 208, take the Goffle Road-Ridgewood/Midland Park exit. Circle down onto Goffle Road and continue straight two miles to Paterson Avenue on the left.

Bartson Fabrics. 240 Glen Avenue (at corner of Rubble Street). (201)652-3664. This is a mill end shop chock-full of designer upholstery and drapery fabrics in bolts. Three rooms worth! Heavy cotton chintz in prints, stripes, and florals, toiles, matelasse, chenilles, and more. They have quantities of overstock from Robert Allen, Waverly, Old Deerfield, and other fine manufacturers. Prices as low as $3.50 per yard.

Brownstone Mill Antique Center. 11 Paterson Avenue. (201)445-3074. This antique center houses 20 shops in a quaint setting. Mostly smalls, but some furniture. The Linen Closet upstairs has magnificent tablecloths, from formal ones to kitschy ones from the '40s with state maps. The antique center is open only Wednesday through Saturday, 10:30 a.m. to 5 p.m.

SECAUCUS

The factory outlet business in the United States is huge, and Hartz Mountain Industries led the industry when it established Secaucus as a warehouse and retail outlet center in the 1970s. A number of garment center manufacturers like Donna Karan and Liz Clairborne, importers, and catalog operations have their warehouses in New Jersey and can offer rock-bottom prices on overstocks, returns, and samples because trucking fees are virtually nil. Quality at Secaucus ranges from the sublime to the sad, so be careful. But bring money, because sometimes bargains are too good to pass up. My feeling is that Secaucus is not as good as it used to be. Some of the best outlets, like the higher end Calvin Klein or the Isaac Mizrahi bridge line, have closed or moved to

Woodbury Common in Spring Valley, NY.

Directions: *From the Garden State Parkway,* get off at Exit 153/Route 3 East. Ride about 5 miles. Cross the Hackensack River and get off at the Meadowlands Parkway. All outlets are located off the Meadowlands Parkway.

From the New Jersey Turnpike Western Extension, exit at 16W. After toll, follow Route 120 East to outlets area.

From the New Jersey Turnpike Eastern Extension, get off at 16E/Lincoln Tunnel. After paying your toll, do not get on Route 495 but stay straight where it says "Secaucus." At the first light, turn left on Paterson Plank Road and go two blocks to the light at County Avenue. Turn left on County Avenue and go past the UPS depot to the light at Secaucus Road. Turn right on Secaucus Road and the first outlets will be on your left.

For the shops and restaurants of Harmon Meadows Boulevard, take the Meadowland Parkway to Route 3 East, then exit at Harmon Meadows Boulevard. Park near the Marriott and movie theaters. From Meadowland Parkway, take Route 3 East service road, turn right at Sunoco Station, go to light at Paterson Plank Road and turn right.

Strategies: Because the outlet area is crowded on weekends, a weekday excursion might allow unhurried shopping with few crowds. Good news: this is not Bergen County, so all stores are open Sunday from noon to about 5 or 6 p.m. Late night is Thursday. Pick one outlet "mall" or group of stores, such as the Designer Outlet Gallery at 55 Hartz Way, and park there. When you have shopped all the stores in the area, drive to a different area and shop there. When you are at the outlets, you are close to New Jersey's premier sports complex, the Meadowlands, located on Route 3 West. Couple your shopping trip with dinner and an evening athletic event such as basketball, hockey, or soccer.

BEST SHOPPING

Brownstone Studio Fashion Outlet. 10 Enterprise Avenue. (201)601-9711. Many women love this catalog, and here you will find the overstock at incredible savings. Summery clothes in silky, cool fabrics; loungewear; and easy-to-wear dresses from Wilroy. Many plus sizes. Also shoes, hats, earrings, and other accessories.

Banister Shoe Studio. 20 Enterprise Avenue (in the Harmon Cove Outlet Center). (201)866-3032. Nine West runs this outlet, which features shoes from Pappagallo, Nine West, Bandolino, and Easy Spirit, among others.

Charles Jourdan Shoes. 20 Enterprise Avenue (in the Harmon Cove Outlet Center). (201)319-1300. Some of the most fashionable men's and women's shoes from France are sold in this outlet at greatly reduced prices. Stock is about a season behind.

Lenox Factory Outlet. 20 Enterprise Avenue (in the Harmon Cove Outlet Center). (201)319-1980. This is a good place for engaged couples because you can pick out your Lenox and Gorham china, crystal, silver, and stainless in one visit. The outlet carries all the Lenox patterns, much of it 20 to 40 percent off list. With vases, frames, and serving pieces, savings can be as much as 60 percent.

Kenneth Cole Company Store. 25 Enterprise Avenue (at the corner of American Way). (201)319-0140. Outlet prices on the trend-setting shoes and leather accessories Kenneth Cole has made famous. Chic clothing as well.

Mikasa Factory Store. 25 Enterprise Avenue. (201)867-3517. Much larger than Mikasa's other New Jersey outlets, this warehouse-sized space carries dozens of china patterns and crystal at 20 to 60 percent off. Glassware, serving pieces, clocks, vases, placemats, and unusual items also grace the shelves. Semi-annual sales are in May and September.

European Designer Outlet. 30 Enterprise Avenue. (201)863-9198. Men get the bulk of the selection here, with suits and sportcoats from top Italian designers such as Giorgio Armani and Valentino. A lot of ties, sweaters, sportswear, and shirts from Joseph Abboud and Andrew Fezza. Women will be pleased to find Armani suits and some excellent pieces by French couturier Ungaro. Several racks of Italian designer blazers, skirts, and pants bearing the Saks Fifth Avenue label were spied recently.

Eileen Fisher Outlet. 60 Enterprise Avenue. (201)866-0300. The comfortable contemporary cotton knits of Eileen Fisher are sold at deep discounts at this new factory outlet. Also look for separates with coordinating tops and skirts or pants.

Searle. 85 Enterprise Avenue (at the corner of Secaucus Road). (201)348-4440. Searle makes the best women's raincoats (sold in Bergdorf Goodman), and the warehouse is stocked with silk-lined and unlined coats about 30 percent off. But prices are still high, about $400 to $500. The shearling coats in colors are exquisite and some can be bought at sizable reductions. The warehouse also carries Donald Pliner shoes and long, luxurious chenille scarves and shawls in jeweltone colors.

Calvin Klein Company Store. 45 Meadowlands Parkway (in the Harmon Cove Outlet Center). (201)319-1856. This store carries the designer's medium-priced sportswear line for women and men. Nice coats and jackets in melton cloth. In summer, look for women's cotton tops and lightweight skirts and pants that go with them.

Gucci. 50 Hartz Way. (201)392-2670. Outlet for Gucci leathers, luggage, shoes, and clothing. Most of the women's shoes available in the outlet are in sample sizes, except during sales when boxes and boxes are shipped in. Scarves are usually plentiful as are handbags, mostly of the summer variety, that didn't sell in the stores. Dark-colored leathers, especially the blacks and the rich browns, get snapped up almost as soon as they come in. Styles are very current. Luggage, butter-soft leather briefcases, and picture frames are usually in stock. Hundreds of wallets, which always make nice gifts. Gucci's sales are wonderful, so get on the mailing list. Sales are held right before major holidays, such as Labor Day and Thanksgiving.

Emanuel. **55 Hartz Way (in the Designer Outlet Gallery). (201)863-5095.** This store carries Ungaro's bridge line and you'll find lots of nice silk suits, shells, and pants that are good for work or dress.

Episode. **55 Hartz Way (in the Designer Outlet Gallery). (201)223-6666.** The clothing in this outlet store is geared for fashion-conscious women in their 20s and 30s. The suits are excellent and so are the slip dresses and sheaths that can go to nighttime parties. Look for the delicate Italian-made bras, slips, teddies, and other lingerie of La Perla, which is carried in Berdorf's and Saks Fifth Avenue. Bras in the $100 range are half off or more.

Joan & David. **55 Hartz Way (in the Designer Outlet Gallery). (201)392-1920.** Although this company has other outlets, this store is perhaps the best stocked with shoes for women and men. All shoes are from the previous year, but designer Joan Helpern does many carry-over designs, so you will not be out of fashion if you buy here. Most shoes are $109, but periodic sales drive this price down. The store has beautifully made tailored clothing from Italy, about half off what the company charges in one of its full-priced stores.

Nahdree/He-Ro. **55 Hartz Way (in the Designer Outlet Gallery). (201)865-1363.** Glitter and glitz fill up this large evening-clothes showroom where Oleg Cassini's Black Tie formal wear for women in long and short editions and Niteline fancy dresses hang with couturier knock-offs by Victor Costa.

Natori. 600 Secaucus Road. (201)553-1348. Almost the whole line can be found here, from the elegance of a Natori peignoir set to the more casual, less expensive Josie line. Silky bras and matching underwear, panty hose, and more sturdy undergarments by Lily of France at prices about half of what you might find in a department store.

Syms. Syms Way (near the intersection of Enterprise Avenue and Emerson Way behind Harmon Cove Outlet Center). (201)902-0300. Educated consumers flock here for the automatic markdowns. Lanz of Austria flannel nightgowns for women and girls at about two-thirds off, Eve Stillman lingerie, Liz Claiborne sportswear for women, Missoni blazers, and Escada and other designer perfumes. Ralph Lauren oxford cloth button-down shirts for men were recently 50 percent below retail. A **Final 1/3 Syms** store is now open next door where clothing for men, women, and children is one-third the original Syms price. Current style men's suits sold nationally for $350 are as low as $66 here. The women's stuff looks a bit dated, but the annex is great for kids' clothes.

Wanna Play. 10-16 Aquarium Drive. (201)863-1234. The wooden swings and playforts are appealing, but it is the selection of discount Little Tikes plastic playthings that draws the crowds of buyers at Christmas time. Other company locations are on Route 46 in Parsippany and Route 1 in South Brunswick.

 **EATS and TASTY TAKEOUT**

Bazookas. 457 Harmon Meadows Boulevard. (201)223-1234. Scrumptious chicken wings served Buffalo style, with celery sticks and blue cheese dressing, plus burgers and grills. The bar is excellent for sports (and people) watching.

Bristol Cafe. 55 Hartz Way (in the Designer Outlet Gallery). (201)271-0062. For a quick lunch stop – designer sandwiches like chicken and arugula, with pastry and brownies to accompany. Also cappuccino to go.

China Chef. 1322 Paterson Plank Road. (201)348-6386. An excellent Hong Kong style lunch, with dim sum served every day.

SUMMIT

Many New Jerseyans who prefer town living rather than suburbia say they'd like to live in Summit more than anyplace else. This is an all-American town with wide avenues, large turn-of-the-century homes with circular driveways, a convenient train for commuters, and a spectacular town center with a wide variety of shopping and dining possibilities. Located within shouting distance of The Mall at Short Hills, Summit stores have been forced to become inventive. They carry high-end merchandise that one does not find in the department stores or the chains. Should you tire of shopping, Summit's serene Reeves-Reed Arboretum has nearly 13 acres of formal gardens and is open year-round. The Arboretum is located at 165 Hobart Avenue, (908)273-8787. Also interesting are the galleries in the New Jersey Center for Visual Arts, 68 Elm Street, (908)273-9121.

Directions: *From New Jersey Turnpike* and Garden State Parkway, head west on I-78 local lanes. Get off on Route 24 West and exit where it says Summit Avenue, Summit. At the traffic light, turn left onto Summit Avenue. This will carry you into town. Springfield Avenue is the main thoroughfare.

If you are heading East on I-78 from Somerset and Union counties, get off at the Glenside Avenue exit. Turn left at the traffic light and follow Glenside to the stop sign at the Morris Avenue intersection. This is a bit of a dangerous intersection, so watch the traffic on Morris Avenue carefully. Turn left onto Morris Avenue and travel past the Overlook Hospital to Summit Avenue. Turn right onto Summit Avenue and go the two long blocks to Springfield Avenue.

Strategies: Summit is a walking town. Park once, but please feed the meter because the police are very diligent in this town. Best parking is across from the train station on Union Place. When you have finished browsing, get in the car and head up Springfield Avenue, past Winberie's, to Morris Avenue. Turn right onto Morris and head for the Summit Antiques Center and shops on the outskirts.

 **BEST SHOPPING**

Siegel's Stationery Shop. 379 Springfield Avenue. (908)273-2340. A Staples or an Office Max cannot duplicate the rich smell of leather office accessories, the richness of fabric-covered albums for photos, or the feel of fine writing instruments. Siegel's is the ultimate stationery store. Paper, invitations, cards, school supplies, and gifts for the executive. You'll never have to wait for a salesperson here!

Adobe East. 445 Springfield Avenue. (908)273-8282. This shop has moved around suburban Essex County and finally landed in Summit. Terrific Native American items and art from the Southwest. Lovely silver jewelry and pottery.

Jos. A. Bank Clothier. 447 Springfield Avenue.

(908)273-6633. A men's clothing store where everything is preppy and affordable. Perfect for late teen and college-aged youngsters and for their fathers. Suits, sports clothing, nice shirts.

Persnickety. 447 Springfield Avenue. (908)522-0100. See Ridgewood entry for a description.

Creative Works. 474 Springfield Avenue. **(908)598-0955.** The two women who are the designers here are very fanciful and clever. They create interior accents with dried and silk flowers. Lots of ready-made options in the small shop behind Springfield Avenue. Or bring in an idea and color scheme and they'll make one up special for you.

Cove Discount Carpet. 487 Springfield Avenue. (908)273-0220. A family business run by the Freda siblings, Donna, Tommie, and Lori, Cove boasts the widest range of carpets in New Jersey, from $10 a yard industrial grade carpet for the basement (that actually looks good) to $150 a yard Wiltons and Axminsters imported from England. Custom area rugs are their specialty. Very professional sales staff.

Elephantales. 26 Maple Street. (908)277-6834. A toy store that makes you happy just to be in it. Educational toys, books, dolls, games.

Gamelan Shop. 39 Maple Street. (908)273-4445. The owners love all things Balinese and they have stocked this shop with the best of Asian arts and crafts. Very interesting gifts, children's toys, fabrics.

Marie Stadler Inc. 20 Woodland Avenue. (908)522-0252. Summit's best store for ladies' apparel. They carry sportswear and suits but are best known for evening wear and mother-of-the-bride outfits. Lots in stock, but Stadler's also will order for you. Great customer service.

Paperfolio. 4 Beechwood Road. (908)277-0459. Invitations for parties and celebrations, wonderful cards, and a great selection of papers and picture frames. This is a place where the art of writing is still very much respected (note the pens).

Plumquin. 12 Beechwood Road. (908)273-3425. A decorating and gift shop where everything is put together smashingly. Antiques abound, in addition to lovely painted furniture.

The Summit Antiques Center. 511 Morris Avenue. (908)273-9373. Open daily. A story and a half with 30 dealers and stock that changes week to week. Mostly from local estate sales, the stock largely consists of furniture and china, but you will also find jewelry, paintings, clocks, and postcards.

 EATS and TASTY TAKEOUT

JB Winberie Restaurant & Bar. 2 Kent Place Boulevard. (908)277-4224. This restaurant, located in the town's old opera house, puts you at ease the minute you walk in. You know the type of place – big bar, dark woods, and televisions high on the wall. Great for burgers and onion rings, caesar salads, and lighter fare.

Summit Diner. 1 Union Place. (908)277-3256. How can you pass up this trolley-car-shaped little diner which has been in Summit since 1929? Dark wood walls, marble counters, and tile floors make this a throwback to a time when, in America, the diner was the epitome of trendiness. Breakfast is heavenly, lunch pretty basic – burgers, sandwiches, and french fries.

Souffle. 7 Union Place. (908)598-0717. Food from the sunny Mediterranean. Lunch, weekdays only, consists of salads, grills, and omelets. Expensive, but a delightful repast. No liquor license.

SHORTER SHOPPING TRIPS in NORTHERN NEW JERSEY

BOONTON

A gritty, industrial hill town which adjoins some of New Jersey's toniest suburbs, Boonton is trying to reinvent itself as an antique capital. There are about 12 shops up and down Main Street, about five concentrated at the bottom of the hill and the rest after the traffic light. Call (973)334-4416 for information.

Directions: Take Route 80 West to Route 287 North, get off at Exit 44-A, circle around back over the highway and head straight on Route 511 (Main Street).

 **BEST SHOPPING**

Remembrance of Things Past. 315 Main Street. (973)402-9421. A jumbled shop, but if it's

Victoriana you want, Nancy has the best. Silver, china, decorative items, Roseville, and a great selection of salesmen's samples in furniture and hardware. Always in stock: antique inkwells and shaving paraphernalia that would make a unique gift for a man.

Blue Shutters Antiques. 321 Main Street. **(973)299-1344.** Owner Anne Wool has lots of lamps, interesting jewelry, English bone china, and majolica, as well as tea sets and other service pieces in silverplate.

Karl's Antiques and Imports. 502 Main Street. **(973)263-9162.** Elaborate antique furniture and decorative items from France, Germany, and elsewhere. Nothing country here.

Claire Ann's Antiques. 815 and 904 Main Street. **(973)334-2421.** At these two shops under one ownership, you'll find lots of smalls at good prices and furniture such as Hoosier cabinets, cupboards, breakfronts, and Empire sofas. Also, kitchenware from the '30s and '40s, Fiestaware, Roseville, and old toys.

CARLSTADT

This is the Meadowlands area, and there are some unique shopping opportunities hidden among the industrial warehouses and factories.
Directions: To reach Broad Street, take Route 17 South to Paterson Plank Road exit and turn left onto Paterson Plank Road. Go past the Fairfield Inn and turn right onto 20th Street. Come to a stop sign and turn right on Broad Street.
To reach Michele Place from Route 3, get off on Route 120 North. It becomes Route 503. Turn right onto Paterson Plank Road East and make a left onto Michele Place.

To reach Michele Place from Route 17 South, exit on Paterson Plank Road East in Carlstadt to Route 503. Follow sign for Paterson Plank Road East, and make first left onto Michele Place.

BEST SHOPPING

Men's Designer Clothing Warehouse. 60 Broad Street. (201)935-6939. A division of George Weintraub & Sons, Inc., the outlet carries handsome suits, sport coats, topcoats, and tuxedos, all at prices considerably under what the finer stores would be charging for the same merchandise.

Rosenthal China Warehouse Outlet. 355 Michele Place. (201)842-1400. Giftware and magnificent dinnerware from Germany with stemware to match the china patterns. If you don't see what you want in stock, you may order from the catalog. Open Tuesday to Thursday, 10:30 a.m. to 3:30 p.m., and on the last Saturday of every month, from 11 a.m. to 3 p.m.

CLIFTON

Clifton is a primarily residential area dotted with small strip shopping centers where there are some stores of great quality. Corrado's, one of New Jersey's great food shopping experiences, is here.

Directions: For the Bloomfield Avenue stores, take Route 3 and get off at the Bloomfield Avenue/Clifton exit. Stores will be on your right after the first traffic light.

To the Main Avenue area via the Garden State Parkway, heading northbound on the Garden

State, get off at Exit 155/Hazel Street. At the stop sign, make a left. Take your first right. The stores are at the bottom of the hill.

To reach Main Avenue from Route 46 East, take the Piaget Avenue exit, turn left onto Main Avenue heading north, and go toward the Garden State Parkway. Stores will be on the right.

 **BEST SHOPPING**

Brava. 1053 Bloomfield Avenue (adjacent to the Rowe-Manse Emporium, around the back of a small shopping center on the lower level underneath Bernie's children's clothing). (973)777-1385. This is one of the best discount stores in New Jersey for top-of-the-line women's clothing and accessories. Well-stocked with Armani, Moschino's Cheap and Chic Line, Max Mara, Ralph Lauren couture, and Nicole Miller. They carry some suits, dresses, and outerwear, but mostly separates. The costume jewelry department is outstanding, with Bakelite pieces from the 1930s displayed amidst contemporary M. and J. Savitt beaded necklaces and bracelets. Some nice handbags, including Moschino and Kate Spade, a Prada look-alike.

The Rowe-Manse Emporium. 1065 Bloomfield Avenue. (973)472-8170. A most unusual place, a kind of department store of gifts, with big displays of unusual items for Valentine's Day, Easter, and Christmas. Everyone loves Rowe-Manse – they even love the name!

Just Coats. 1500 Main Avenue. (973)772-3575. This outlet is located in an old red brick factory where you will find well-made melton wool full-length coats and peacoats from manufacturers such as Larry Levine and others. Also, raincoats, swimwear, and sportswear. Look for great bargains at their semi-annual tent sales.

Corrado's Family Affair Gourmet Market. 1578 Main Avenue. (973)340-0628. Before there were "box stores," there was Corrado's, as big as a ballfield under cover and crammed with gourmet and ethnic foods, produce, cheeses, meats, baked goods, sauces, and crackers. Prices outdo any supermarket. Open every day at 5 a.m., closing at 9 or 10 p.m., depending upon the day.

GARFIELD

Shoppers don't normally flock to Garfield, an industrial community on the banks of the Passaic River. But those who use fabrics for home sewing and home furnishing make this a regular stop.

Directions: *From Route 80,* get off at Exit 61/Elmwood Park. At the traffic light at the bottom of the exit, turn right onto River Road. Go 1 mile to the Gulf Station and turn left on Lanza Avenue.

 **BEST SHOPPING**

Fabric Buyers Inc. 181 Lanza Avenue. **(973)546-4466.** Look for overstocks and mill ends of fine fabrics for home decorating and sewing. Some are on rollers at the store entrance. Others are stacked on racks in no particular order or colorway. Dress goods included glitzy fabrics for costume-making. In upholstery and drapery fabrics, I saw goods from Schumacher, Waverly, Jay Yang, and some Fortuny-like Italian imports. Brocades were particularly nice. Those who like the hunt will delight to dig here. Open Wednesday to Saturday.

RIDGEFIELD PARK

Crystal Outlet. 2 Bergen Turnpike (near Route 46). (201)440-4200. Open just two times a year, early to mid-December and early to mid-May, this crystal wholesaler has fantastic sales. The best brands of lead crystal, lamps, ceramics, and wedding favors. Call to get on the list and the company will send a postcard notifying you of the sale days.

WAYNE, TOTOWA, and CEDAR GROVE

Off Route 46 and tucked back along the industrial roads that lead from it are a number of fine outlets shoppers are sure to enjoy.

Directions: *To Riverview Drive factory outlets from Route 46 West,* exit at Riverview Drive/Little Falls. Go up the ramp and at the first light, bear left, then make a right onto Riverview Drive. Home Depot will be on the left. Go straight past 5 traffic lights.

From Route 46 East, get off at the Riverview Drive/Wayne exit, circle over Route 46, then go straight past 6 traffic lights.

For Hanes Drive, turn left on Edison Drive at the Shell station. The road will curve left, becoming Hanes Drive.

To Cedar Grove, take Route 80 to Route 23 South. In Cedar Grove, turn left on Commerce Way just before the big Presbyterian church.

BEST SHOPPING
WAYNE

Mayer-Berkshire Outlet. **Hanes Drive and Edison Drive. (973)696-6204.** Excellent quality Berkshire pantyhose and socks are 30 percent off, and close-outs run as little as $2. Also Lee jeans, Joe Boxer sportswear, Hot Sox, sweats for the whole family, and men's socks such as Calvin Klein, Ralph Lauren, and Gold Toe, about 25 percent off.

BEST SHOPPING
TOTOWA

The Down Home Pillow and Comforter Factory Outlet. **85 Route 46 West (behind Hillman Eyes and next to Petco). (973)812-8100 or 1-800-ALL-DOWN.** Bloomingdale's and other department stores known for their white goods have their private brand pillows and comforters made here and so can you – at half the price of retail. Choose from different weights in down, feather, silk, and even wool comforters. Bed pillows come in boudoir, neck roll, standard, queen, and king, with various gradients of fill. If you have fabric and want to make your own pillow covers, Down Home has the pillows to fit inside or will make custom sizes. If they are not busy, the filling can be done while you wait. This store has a winter clearance sale in late February when prices are slashed 30 to 50 percent.

Perugina Outlet Store. **25 Madison Road. (973)890-0115.** Italian-made chocolates, packed for gift giving at prices considerably under retail. Also Baci cookies, pasta sauces, and other Italian delicacies. Closed Sunday and Monday except during the Christmas season. Note: There is a second Perugina Outlet Store, located at 370 Market Street in Saddle Brook, (201)843-4200. It carries just chocolates, with the largest selection available before Christmas and Easter.

 **BEST SHOPPING**

CEDAR GROVE

Old Deerfield Fabrics. **99** Commerce Road. **(973)239-6600.** Old Deerfield's outlet for seconds and overages, which was called Stonehenge, closed in December 1997. However, the company intends to open to the public for occasional sales. Look for advertisements in the Star-Ledger. Old Deerfield offers roomfuls of fabrics, separated by color and by drapery or upholstery weight. Some handsome Ralph Lauren fabrics, also Schumacher and Bloomcraft.

CENTRAL
NEW JERSEY

CHESTER

Once an iron mining boomtown, Chester lost its importance in the latter 19th century and stayed a quiet country town until 20 years ago when folks began to restore the commercial buildings and homes along Main Street and turn them into restaurants and shops for antiques, clothing, and home furnishings. It's easy meandering and the shops are low-key. Nothing is outrageously expensive. A shopping excursion to Chester, together with a ride to adjacent Mendham, makes a fine day of recreational shopping. Prior to Halloween, some of the local farms like Riamede on Oakdale Road off Route 206 North, (908)879-5353, host apple and pumpkin picking, complete with orchard hayrides and activities for children.

Directions: Take I-78 to Route 287 North. Get off at the second exit, 22-B, which says Route 202-206/Bedminster. At the second traffic light, Route 206 goes off to the left. Take that 9 miles to Chester. At the traffic light at Route 206 and Route 24, turn right onto Route 24 East, which is Main Street.

From I-80 West, get off at Exit 27A/Route 206 South, and go 7 miles to Chester. Turn left onto Route 24 East (Main Street).

From the Morristown area, take Route 24 West to Chester.

Strategies: Most of Chester's quaint shops are along Main Street from Route 206 to the traffic light at Ironia Road. There is usually plenty of on-street parking, either along Main Street or on the streets that branch off from it. In addition, there are free parking lots behind all the stores as well as one behind the Publick House. Don't forget the stores on Route 206 in Chester Shopping Center (look for the Shop-Rite) or the Chester Mall on the western side of Main.

 **BEST SHOPPING**

Alstede Farms. 84 Route 24 West (at Pleasant Hill Road). (908)879-7189. Open year-round, 7 days a week. Alstede is a farm market that grows fabulous fruits and vegetables on its 800 acres and fills in with the best of Jersey-grown produce. Flowers, annuals, perennials.

The Beauty of Civilization. 30 Main Street (back along Perry Street). (908)879-2044. An eclectic group shop with antique and Bakelite jewelry, vintage clothes, and smalls. Lots of choices.

Kid N' Kaboodle. 38 Main Street. (908)879-2919. A fun store for kids and their parents. Gaily-colored furniture for the toddler set, accessories, clothes, and personalized gifts.

Summerfield's Antique Furniture Warehouse. 44 Main Street (in the back at the edge of the parking lot). (908)879-9020. Large selection of refurbished antique furniture for the living room, dining room, and bedroom. Also home furnishings and accessories.

Clothes Call. 58 Main Street. (908)879-4130. For a small store, a large selection of chic, comfortable women's apparel and accessories. Designers like Joan Vass, Eileen Fisher, and Sarah Arizona plus the fabled sweaters of Putamayo.

Pegasus Antiques. 98 Main Street. (908)879-4792. Accessories and decorator items. Thousands of them.

Marita Daniels Antiques. 127 Main Street. (908)879-6488. A general line of antiques, with lots of interesting items for the garden.

Chester House Antiques. 294 East Main Street. (908)879-4331. An old colonial crammed with Fiestaware, vintage clothing, exquisite antiques, linens, art, and accessories.

Black River Trading Company. 15 Perry Street. **(908)879-6778.** If Chester has an early American feel, this shop goes delightfully against the grain, with a Sante Fe kind of flavor. They stock antique furniture, bed linens in natural fabrics, crafts, candles in dreamy colors, antique jewelry, and gifts.

Chester Antique Center. 32 Grove Street. (908)879-4331. Houses several shops, including **Elaine Morsch** and **Once Upon A Time.**

Jantiques. 10 Budd Avenue. (908)879-9409. A large selection of glass, china, and antique lamps, but the shop also does upholstery, caning, and lamp rewiring. They have a huge inventory in a warehouse nearby, so if you don't see what you want, ask.

Mangel's Homemade Candies. 115 Route 206. (908)879-5640. Scrumptious chocolates all made the old-fashioned way. Everything is very fresh.

 EATS and TASTY TAKEOUT

Larison's Turkey Farm Inn. 2 West Main Street. (908)879-5521. Practically an institution in Chester, Larison's is busiest at Thanksgiving but never takes off its menu a family-style all-American roast turkey lunch with all the fixings. Housed in an inn dating back to the early 19th century. If the kids' interest wanes, take them to see the farm animals on the grounds.

Publick House Restaurant and Inn. 111 Main Street. (908)879-6878. This was the original stagecoach stop in town. The food is standard American fare. In summer and early fall, ask for a table outdoors.

Sally Lunn's. 15 Perry Street. (908)879-7731. A restaurant-tearoom cum antique shop, this beautifully decorated import straight from the English countryside has charm and the highest-quality foods. Everything is made from scratch, including the soups, the breads, the Cornish pasties, and Helen's famous chicken potpie. At tea, scones made from a secret recipe are served warm, with strawberry jam and clotted cream.

WORTH a DETOUR
MENDHAM

Directions: Mendham, an upscale village of colonial character, is several miles east of Chester on Route 24.

Diane Smith Quality Consignments. 1 Hilltop Road. (973)543-6199. Come and browse here. Quality estate items on sale, including dinner sets glassware, furniture, jewelry, and designer clothes. Changing stock — you never know what you'll find.

Katydids Boutique. 6 East Main Street. (973)543-1770. This well-lit, attractive store with high ceilings just moved from Route 202, Morristown. Silk flower arrangements, fine crafts suitable for gift giving, and home furnishings. A large selection, excellent sales help.

EATS and TASTY TAKEOUT

Black Horse Inn and Pub. 1 West Main Street. (973)543-7300. A great place for lunch, decorated a la horse country. The food is well prepared and diners can always select from a bounteous buffet. Visit the restaurant shop for the finest in gourmet foods and gifts.

The Place in Mendham. 3 East Main Street. (973)543-9781. It's where the whole town goes, from construction workers to fancy ladies in tennis whites. However, the hours are rather restricted — 7 a.m. to 3 p.m. weekdays and 8 a.m. to 2 p.m. Saturdays.

FLEMINGTON

Flemington's historic monuments, such as the courthouse where Bruno Richard Hauptmann stood trial for the killing of the Lindbergh baby and the Victorian-era buildings on Main Street, sit side by side with some of the best outlet shopping in America. More than enough to see and do for a whole day.

Directions: *West on Route 78 to Route 287 South.* Travel on Route 287 South about two miles and exit at Route 202-206 South/Bridgewater-Somerville. Stay on Route 202 South as it cuts over the Somerville Circle and drive 11 miles to Flemington. At the traffic light at Church Street (the sign will say Flemington Business Center), take a right and cross over Route 31 to Main Street. Turn right for Main Street shopping; go straight for Liberty Village outlets.

Another route is to go straight on Route 202 South past the Church Street traffic light and go around the Flemington Circle. There are a few outlets just off the circle. Take Route 12 South about a quarter-mile and park in the lots there for Liberty Village and the Feed Mill. You can walk into Liberty Village from there.

Other outlets are beyond the circle on Route 202-31 North, but you will have to take a jughandle at the Raritan Avenue/Commerce Street exit of Route 202-31 South to reach them.

If you are coming from I-95 and the South Jersey-Trenton area, take Route 31 North to Flemington. Use the Flemington Circle to get into town.

Strategies: Shoppers can park once for the principal outlets, but to hit Mikasa, Le Creuset,

Flemington Cut Glass, and the restaurants on Main Street, you will have to drive into the center of town. Outlets and shops are open daily. Avoid big weekend crowds by shopping during the week. If you want to combine shopping with an old-fashioned steam train excursion, catch the Black River & Western Railroad at Turntable Junction where the railroad tracks run through the shopping area. On Saturdays and Sundays in warmer weather, the train goes to Ringoes and Lambertville. Runs are at 11:30 a.m., 1 p.m., 2:30 p.m., and 4 p.m. Pick up a complimentary Shopping in Flemington Guide when you hit the outlets. In the guide are coupons for use at select stores.

 **BEST SHOPPING**

Cambridge Dry Goods Outlet Store. 31A Liberty Village (on Church Street outside the complex). (908)788-1999. The best cotton knit skirts and pants at terrific prices. Conservative clothing with little nod to trends. Cotton sweaters with intricate embroidery are always on the racks.

Jones New York. 32, 33, 46, and 78 Liberty Village. (908)782-0082. If you are a Jones New York fanatic, you can bliss out at Liberty Village's four Jones stores! Two carry casual clothing in misses and large sizes. Another is for sport looks. Jones Executive Suite specializes in looks women and men can wear to work. The suit prices are excellent: two suits for $350, normally $220 each. There are ties, shirts, and dresses, as well. The Saville brand is also available here.

Calvin Klein Company Store. 43 Liberty Village. (908)788-1611. This outlet carries mostly Klein's less expensive CK line. Good jeans and tops for men and women and some ladies' suits.

Le Gourmet Chef. 44 Liberty Village. (908)782-

7879. The shop has cookware and ingredients, but it is best known for stocking items that can go into do-it-yourself gift baskets. Just buy a load of shredded paper and go to town, filling your basket with the best of oils, vinegars, designer cookies, candy, and ethnic foods such as Mexican picante sauce. Throw in a few potholders, utensils, a candle or two, and you have a fabulous gift for not nearly as much as you'd spend by buying a ready-made basket.

Donna Karan Company Store. 50 Liberty Village. (908)806-3754. This huge store carries last year's merchandise, but you will find nice ladies' business suits, sportswear, good sunglasses, and expensive handbags at substantial discounts.

Euro Bebe. 53 Liberty Village. (908)806-4688. This shop carries the finest in French clothing for infants and toddlers. Petit Bateau, Petit Faune, and Pomme Framboise are the chief brands. Stretchies from these companies will last 100 washings and still look new.

Limited Editions for Her. 56 Liberty Village. (908)788-5352. If you are a devotee of the Carlisle Collection, an exclusive brand of ladies' suits and separates sold privately in representatives' homes, shop here for last year's styles. Carlisle is classic clothing, so the designs do not change all that much, which makes this an excellent place to shop for cocktail clothing. Carlisle uses rich fabrics, trims, and silks in its shells.

Joan & David. 57 Liberty Village. (908)788-0515. See Secaucus entry for a description.

Anne Klein Factory Store. 60 Liberty Village (facing the pond). (908)782-9646. This shop carries the whole line, including suits, separates, dresses, and accessories. Some very nice buys.

Polo Ralph Lauren Factory Store. 66 Liberty Village. (908)284-2954. This huge outlet carries a wide range of clothing and home furnishings. Look for good buys on seconds in Lauren's stock-in-trade, the polo shirt. Also, designer women's suits and dresses.

Brooks Brothers Factory Store. 75B Liberty Village (at the junction of the main shopping street and the pond). (908)788-4858. Brooks Brothers has great sportswear and sportcoats for both men and women. There are always luscious sweaters at holiday time and the array of summer tops and shorts is extensive.

Tommy Hilfiger. 76 Liberty Village. (908)782-1150. This designer outlet also carries a wide range of sport separates, including playful sweaters, outerwear, and pants for dress down, school, or even golf. Very jaunty looking stuff.

Nautica. 77 Liberty Village. (908)806-3911. This store has the looks that appeal to young male Generation X-ers. Sweats, tees, pants, hats, all bearing the vaunted Nautica name. A direct competitor with Polo for young people's dollars.

Waterford-Wedgwood Outlet. 82 Liberty Village. (908)782-6568. An excellent location for gifts, the store carries the best in Irish crystal, lamps, and jam jars. A plus is the classic Wedgwood china that has the versatility to fit in with modern or traditional home furnishings.

Ellen Tracy. 86 Liberty Village (at the end of the main shopping street toward Route 12). (908)806-8177. This Ellen Tracy outlet has very current merchandise, including coordinated looks in women's suits, dressy cocktail suits, fancy sweaters, and lots of wonderful shells to wear under suits.

Pfaltzgraff Factory Store. 50 Mine Street. (908)782-2918. Pfaltzgraff occupies the old Stangl Pottery factory. Its earthy brand of everyday dishes and serving platters go in the most contemporary of homes but also mix well with antiques. All the company's patterns, discontinueds and seconds, at discounted prices.

Kitchen Collection. 50 Mine Street (next to Pfaltzgraff). (908)806-2808. A lot of Proctor-Silex appliances at good prices, but the real plus is that they carry Kitchen Aid mixers and blenders that have been factory-refurbished. These are new appliances that have been damaged in shipping to retail stores and have been rebuilt. Savings are 30 percent off what you might be able to get in a department store sale. Lots of good quality cookware and gadgets, too.

Dansk Factory Outlet. Dansk Plaza, Routes 202 & 31 (on the Flemington Circle). (908)782-7077. The most gorgeous wooden salad bowls, imported china, barware, and accoutrements for cooking are packed into this outlet. Save about 60 percent on seconds, overstocks, and discontinued items. A great place for young people setting up housekeeping. A good place to come for bridal shower gifts.

Antiques Emporium. 32 Church Street. (908)782-5077. There are 60 dealers here and you'll find something you like, whatever your fancy – old Stangl, cut glass, jewelry, etc.

Reebok-Rockport Factory Direct Stores. 63 Church Street (two separate stores, connected, in Heritage Place near Route 31). Reebok: (908)806-0287, Rockport: (908)806-0438. When it comes to walking in comfort, we all turn to Rockport, and this outlet has many styles to choose from. Also Reebok sneakers for running, walking, and cross-training.

Bill Healy Crystal. 110 Broad Street. (908) 806-2100. Bill Healy, one of America's master crystal cutters, has stocked his showroom with exquisite items for the home as well as custom gifts. Vases, glasses, chandeliers, and bowls are for sale. Where this shop excels is in the custom gifts category. Healy will design anything and engrave it. There are crystal golf balls for the enthusiast, apples for the teacher, engraved toasting glasses and crystal invitations for weddings, and many unusual awards and trophies. The shop also specializes in the repair and restoration of crystal, particularly chipped stemware. If that fancy Baccarat wine glass chips, bring it in. Healy will restore it so you cannot see where it was chipped.

Cookware & More. 110 Broad Street.

(908)782-1735. Look for Rosenthal China discounted 30 percent on open stock and about 10 percent if ordered. The shop is a direct factory outlet for top-rated All-Clad cookware and Scanpan Non-Stick from Denmark in addition to the Asta line of classic bronze-handled teapots, casseroles, and cookware. There is Wusthof-Trident cutlery at 20 percent off, including its cheaper new Laser line, and the springform pans made by Kaiser of Germany, the best for cheesecake. You can always find some pieces of Apilco fine china from France. Very helpful personnel.

Louie & Lenny. 79 Main Street. (908)788-1942. Packed with fashionable ladies' clothing for work or sport, with a wonderful selection of evening things. The clothes, hand-selected by the owners, are in the contemporary vein and very wearable. A lot of skirts have elastic waists to fit all sizes. Extremely helpful personnel.

Mikasa Factory Store. 95 Main Street. (908)788-3620. See Secaucus entry for a description.

Flemington Cut Glass. 156 Main Street. (908)782-3017. Drive in and park in the rear. This used to be the place where one could see old world artisans cutting glass, but today none of the cutting is done on the premises. The store stocks everything you ever wanted in glass, from everyday ware to the finest cut crystal from Swarovski. Dresden-brand crystal is a German manufacturer that has gone out of business, and Flemington Cut Glass is selling the last of its stock at nice prices. (There are a few older pieces available for sale on the first level.) Goebel figurines are discounted about 15 to 20 percent. So is Queen's-brand china from England. Senior citizens get 10 percent off on Wednesdays.

Le Creuset. 156 Main Street (in the front of Flemington Cut Glass). (908)782-1224. Enameled cast-iron cookware, French-made, in a multitude of colors and sizes. Prices are about 70 percent off retail. The casseroles are great oven-to-table ware. Some aprons and accessories.

Main Street Antique Center. 156 Main Street. **(908)788-6767.** Located next to Cut Glass, this is a group shop for more than 100 dealers whose wares are in booths and glass cases. Quilts, lots of English china and chintzware, even some nice wicker and large pieces of furniture. There are some dealers who specialize in collectibles. On three floors!

Flemington Fur Company. 8 Spring Street. **(908)782-2212.** Thousands of women and men start their fur shopping here and end up buying here because of the great prices and accommodating personnel. All the latest high-style looks in fur, especially mink. They can remake your old fur or take that really aged pelt and turn it into a lining for a trenchcoat. There's rarely been such a large collection under one roof.

 EATS and TASTY TAKEOUT

Canterbury Corner. 25 Turntable Junction (at the corner of Church Street and Central Avenue). **(908)788-5547.** A spot of England in the midst of Flemington. Tea sandwiches and scones with clotted cream for lunch or high tea. They serve some of the most unusual and delicious teas around.

Market Roost. 65 Main Street. **(908)788-4949.** Large, flavorful sandwiches, salads, and lunch specials are on the menu at this downtown eatery near the courthouse. The Market Roost is also one of the region's top caterers, so one will always find marvelous baked goods to go with lunch.

WORTH a DETOUR
RINGOES

Directions: From Flemington, head south on Route 202-31 about 4 miles to Ringoes.

Luggage Factory Outlet. **Highway 202-31 North. (908)788-4810.** The outlet carries standard suitcases, garment bags, suiters, and carry-aboard luggage at strong discounts from manufacturers such as Lark, Boyt, Samsonite, and Travel Pro. Tumi is stocked, but not at a discount. The outlet will usually beat the price in any ad. For kids who are camp-bound, they carry a 52-inch duffle. It takes two hands to handle, but, boy, can it stuff a lot in! Very knowledgeable and pleasant sales help.

FRENCHTOWN

Stretched out along the Delaware River, this charming town has much to recommend it, including the flagship store for Blue Fish, the line of stenciled cotton ladies' clothing that chic women wear when they want to be comfortable. The downtown commercial district underwent a transformation a few years ago when the municipality got a grant to install sidewalks. Within months, upscale new shops had moved in. Frenchtown makes a great day trip, especially toward the end of the week and on weekends when all the shops are open for business. It's never mobbed.

Directions: *From Route 78 West* pick up Route 287 South. Travel on Route 287 South about two miles and exit at Route 202-206

South/Bridgewater-Somerville. Stay on Route 202 South as it cuts over the Somerville Circle and drive 11 miles to Flemington. At the Flemington Circle, follow signs to Route 12. Take Route 12 about 10 miles into the heart of Frenchtown. To get to the shopping district, go left on Race Street, then make a gentle right onto Bridge Street. Street parking.

Strategies: Start at Race Street and walk to the water.

 # BEST SHOPPING

Fiddleheads. 29 Race Street. (908)996-2545. A tasteful shop that crams in the best in home furnishings, garden items, and gifts, many with a French accent. Stunning picture frames, baby items, Barbara Eigen fruit and vegetable pottery. Hard-to-find flexible Danish clogs are among the shop's best-selling items.

Garbo & Sasha. 16 Race Street. (908)996-7976. Heavenly women's clothes are the draw here. Natural fibers, very comfortable. Some tops made of chenille and fabric from the '40s. Cool linen for warmer months. Shop carries interesting accessories like scarves and jewelry and eclectic home furnishings.

Objects of Spirit. 12 Race Street. (908)996-4442. Southwest pottery, twig furniture, Native American items.

Jeanine-Louise Antiques. 8 Race Street. (908)996-3520. Lots of varied items in this 15-year-old antique shop. Some country French pottery. Friendly French proprietor.

Delaware River Trading Co. 47 Bridge Street. (908)996-3447. A garden and home shop with some irresistible goods. Natural fiber bedding, distinctive garden things, great selection of terra cotta pots and the flora that go in them. Unique are the soaps and room sprays.

Variete. 43 Bridge Street. (908)996-7876. With the owner a former Philadelphia caterer who loves to preserve and cook, the shop is stocked with his handsomely packaged homemade jams, vinegars, and mustards. There are also teas, herbs, and honey that is locally gathered. Look for the pickled vidalia onions! Plus French porcelains and pottery, gift items, and crackers from DiCamillo's in Niagara Falls, NY. Buy a papier-mache tray and make up your own gift package.

JH Home. 29 Bridge Street. (908)996-0442. Fancy English and American furniture, originals with some terrific reproductions thrown in. Oriental furniture and ethereal Chinese porcelains.

Brooks Antiques. 24 Bridge Street. (908)996-7161. Americana at its most exciting. This shop has primitives, folk art, furniture, and an array of smalls. It is owned by a mother-daughter team, Dorothy and Abby Brooks, who used to have a shop in Lahaska. Stock changes frequently.

Arcadia. 10 Bridge Street. (908)996-7570. If you are looking for fine crafts from America's best, this is the place to shop. Owner Stephen Thompson stocks everything from Adirondack furniture to delicate glass and pottery. There are fabulous decoupage trays, lamps, and whimsical items.

Blue Fish Clothing. 62 Trenton Avenue (Route 29). (908)996-3720. Fresh as the morning air, this oversized, roomy clothing for women and children makes people smile. Carried in fine stores throughout the United States, the company used to have its headquarters on Sixth Street in Frenchtown. Most of the line can be found in this modern wooden structure set amidst fine plantings. Clothes, shoes, accessories, and scents. Parking on site.

EATS and TASTY TAKEOUT

Frenchtown Inn. 7 Bridge Street. (908)996-3300. In a restored brick structure with a view of the river, the cuisine is nouvelle and well-prepared. Lunch is served Tuesday through Saturday and the Sunday brunch, served from noon to about 3 p.m., is a great way to start a stroll through town. Expensive.

Bridge Cafe. 8 Bridge Street. (908)996-6040. In the red train station before the bridge. They offer excellent sandwiches on homemade breads, creative salads. Baked goods have the best reputation around.

National Hotel. 31 Race Street. (908)996-4871. Facing you as you come down the hill from Route 12 into Frenchtown, this restored tavern is noted for its great bar. Standard American fare — burgers, sandwiches, and salads, plus lots of interesting menu choices. Downstairs is the Rathskeller Pub.

 **WORTH a DETOUR**

OVER the BRIDGE in PENNSYLVANIA

Bucolic Pennsylvania beckons just beyond the Frenchtown shopping district. Cross the narrow bridge and turn left onto Route 32 South and you'll come to Tinicum Park, where there is a superb playground for youngsters and an occasional antiques show on the weekend. Down the road a quarter mile you'll find a complex containing the **River Road Farms** open-air marketplace, **Chachka,** a creative gift shop, and **Two Timers Antiques.** If you turn right onto Route 32 North, in a few miles you'll reach the little hamlet of Upper Black Eddy tucked away off River Road.

EATS and TASTY TAKEOUT

Chef Tell's Manor House. 1800 River Road, Upper Black Eddy, PA (5 miles north of the Frenchtown bridge). (610)982-0212. Part of the empire of the widely known television chef and restaurateur, the Manor House is open for lunch and dinner Wednesday through Saturday and Sunday brunch.

LAMBERTVILLE

Lambertville sprang to life in the early 1700s as a key stopping off place on the Old York Road linking Philadelphia and New York and it became wealthy serving the traveling public. A century later, renewed prosperity came from the locomotive factories and the mills for ceramics and rubber products. Today, the city's fine Federal houses and Victorian mansions provide the backdrop for antique stores, trendy restaurants, and au courant shopping. Many merchants are newcomers; they established themselves in Lambertville when Lahaska and New Hope became too crowded. Lambertville is a delightful place to spend a day. Walkers will find the city most manageable. Tired? Sit on a bench by the river and watch the boats. For a history break, the Marshall House at 62 Bridge Street is open from 1 to 4 p.m. the last weekend of every month, from April to October. Admission is free. The Holcombe-Jimison Farmstead Museum on Route 29 north of Lambertville showcases early farm implements, a rural doctor's office, and a country post office. Open Sunday from 1 to 4 p.m., May to October.

During the last weekend of April, the city celebrates the annual Delaware River shad migration with its fun-filled Shad Fest. There are shad hauling demonstrations, shad dinners, entertainment, and an arts and crafts exhibition.

Directions: *From Route 78 West,* pick up Route 287 South. Travel on Route 287 South about two miles and exit at Route 202-206 South/Bridgewater-Somerville. Stay on Route 202 South as it cuts over the Somerville Circle and drive 11 miles to Flemington. Follow Route 202-31 South around the Flemington Circle and travel beyond Ringoes, about 5 miles. After the Sweet Valley Farms market and the Texaco station on the right, continue straight on Route 202, which becomes more of a superhighway. But please don't speed. There are police all along this road! Get off at the exit that says "Last Lambertville exit/Route 29." Go left at the stop sign, and left again onto Route 29 (North Main Street). Eight or nine blocks on North Main Street will bring you to Bridge Street and the heart of Lambertville.

From the south, take Route 31 North to Route 518 traffic light. Go west on 518 to end (Route 29). Bear right on 29 to traffic light. Take left at light, Bridge Street (Lambertville's main drag.)

Strategies: Head down Bridge Street toward the river, but, just before the bridge, turn right on Lambert Lane and follow it around past the townhouses on the left to Coryell Street. There is usually two-hour metered parking along Coryell Street. Other long-term parking can be found at Kline's Court, located at South Union and Ferry streets. The parking lot at Lambertville Station restaurant on Bridge Street sometimes is available, as well. If you first want to do the flea markets on Route 29 south of town, go early, come back to town to have breakfast, and then walk the shops.

Shopping on foot is easiest. The two main shopping streets are Bridge and North Union Streets. On the north side of town, you won't want to miss Coryell Street, Church Street, and Lambert Lane. On the south side of Bridge Street, check out Main Street. Most shops are open from Thursday to Sunday, with a few open Monday.

Lambertville is one of New Jersey's premier dining spots. Plan to stay for dinner Some of our favorites are Hamilton's Grill Room, Anton's at the Swan, Hertitage Café and charming Manon.

The Delaware and Raritan Canal runs parallel to the Delaware River, and the path alongside it is ideal for walking, running, bicycle riding, and even cross-country skiing in the winter. You can take the path from the bridge adjacent to Lambertville Station restaurant out past Cavallo Park at the end of South Union Street south toward Trenton. Or you might want to try renting in-line skates at Cross-Country Summer Sports Outfitters at 287 South Main Street (Route 29 South) in the Laceworks Complex, (609)397-3366. Boating on the Delaware River (in season) is possible through the Public Boat Launch, a quarter of a mile past the Inn at Lambertville Station on the New Jersey side. New Hope is on the Pennsylvania side of the river, a town chock-full of tourist shops, restaurants, and a regional theater. You will find it more commercial than Lambertville.

 **BEST SHOPPING**

Lambertville Antique Market. Route 29 (1 1/2 miles south of Lambertville). (609)397-0456. Although the colorful antique market is open Wednesday to Sunday, the best days are Saturday and Sunday. More than 100 dealers set up at dawn in this dusty lot, and the earlier you arrive, the better the finds. Many are gone by 1 p.m. The stalls are crammed with everything from art pottery to Barbie dolls from the '60s. In spring and summer, you'll find vendors selling well-priced annuals and perennials. Park on site. You'll find a restaurant on premises and two year-round indoor antique centers, Cobweb, a group shop, and Greywolf.

Golden Nugget Antique Flea Market. Route 29 (next door to the Lambertville Antique Market). (609)397-0811. Same hours as its neighbor. The Golden Nugget features antiques as well as some newer merchandise, annuals and houseplants, and fruits and vegetables. Occasionally, vendors sell dinner-size cloth napkins and tablecloths like those found in fancy stores. Never count on vendors being there from week to week. There is a permanent antique center on the premises.

Bucks County Dry Goods. 285 South Main Street (Route 29 at the Laceworks). (609)397-1288. Women's and men's clothing one might find in department stores at double the price. The accent is on the stylish but comfortable, with brands such as Eileen Fisher, Christy Allen, and Anthropologie. Ideal for teens and the under-30 set.

Gipsy Horse. 287 South Main Street (Route 29 at the Laceworks). (609)397-9359. Known throughout New Jersey as the shop for J. Crew close-outs. They have Crew, Tweeds, and other top catalogue manufacturers, all in season. There is a huge selection, grouped by color. They also carry shoes, umbrellas, and rainwear. Another super place to bring teens.

Lace Factory Outlet. 287 South Main Street (Route 29 at the Laceworks). (609)397-0565. Marvelous selection of laces, trims, and ruffles for professional seamstresses or those attempting their own fashions. Some bridal laces are available. This is the outlet for Towle Laces, which called this plant home for many years. Now Towle makes its lace in North Carolina.

Prestige Antiques. 287 South Main Street (Route 29 at the Laceworks). (609)397-2400. Formal French and English furniture presented by these direct importers. Helpful staff. Armoires come outfitted for television sets and storage needs.

Jim's Antiques, Ltd. 6 Bridge Street. (609)397-7700. Located at the corner of Lambert Lane and Bridge Street, this shop has it all, from English and American silver to bronzes, art glass, American Indian items, and old watches. Also paintings of local scenes.

Park Place Estate and Antique Jewelry. 6 Bridge Street. (609)397-0102. In the same building as Jim's, this inviting shop moved not too long ago from Lahaska. Some unique old pieces, especially the earrings and necklaces. Pearls seem to be a specialty. Some newer stuff from designers like Tiffany and Cartier. Many couples shop for engagement rings here.

Pinch Penny & Dresswell. 10 Bridge Street. (609)397-2229. Carries the Jackeroo line of men's rubberized cotton outerwear from Australia and New Zealand. The handsome range coats and barn jackets merit a close look. Also a line of sportcoats, raincoats, and separates for ladies at discounted prices.

King Charles Ltd. and The Drawing Room. 32 Bridge Street. (609)397-9733. Located in historic, recently renovated Lambertville House. The finest 18th and 19th century English and French antiques, but with a country "Manor House" accent. Lots of accessories. This Princeton transplant carries the most exquisite handmade pillows in the region, and there are almost always two of a kind. Interior design with antiques is a specialty of the company's second shop at 36 South Main Street, (609) 397-7977. The decor is presented in period rooms. Large stock.

The Olde Carriage House. 51 Bridge Street. (609)397-4978. This shop carries unique decorative accessories. Life-sized soft sculptures from "We The People" are $500 and $600. Sculptures have career or sport-hobby themes and can be custom-ordered for gifts.

Mill Crest Antiques. 72 Bridge Street. (609)397-4700. Paula Cooperman is a fabric archivist and her mother, Mickie Rosenberg, is an expert in English and French china and porcelain. Together they run one of the best shops in New Jersey for antique linens, vintage clothing, pillows, quilts, and china sets. The selection of antique tablecloths is spectacular.

Blue Raccoon. 6D Coryell Street (at the front of the Porkyard complex). (609)397-1900. This recently relocated home and garden shop is a feast for the eye! It features garden implements, old and new; topiaries; toile napkins; beautiful sofas and easy chairs; unusual candles; painted country antiques; and other unique stuff collected by the owners Nicholas Bewsey and Nelson Zayas in Indiana, Kentucky, and Ohio. One of the few retailers in New Jersey to carry the ceramics of Barbara Eigen, who is doing polka-dot ice cream bowls, and vases and mugs with nature motifs. Their holiday gifts are outstanding.

Judy Naftulin Antiques. 6 Coryell Street. (609)397-8066. Wire Victorian furniture, garden implements, columns, mercury glass, and other elements of design, from the 18th century to the 20th.

Porkyard Antiques. 8 Coryell Street. (609)397-2088. Beautifully designed co-op antique shop on two levels. Their quilts are wonderful and the country furniture is representative. There is always a lot of Staffordshire.

Kelly McDowell Fine Art & Antiques. 38 Coryell Street. (609)397-4465. The antique Victorian jewelry here is superb and unusual. If you are looking for men's cufflinks or just the right present for that milestone birthday or anniversary, this is the place. Some furniture and accessories.

Joan Evans Antiques. 48 Coryell Street. (609)397-7726. Cutting edge antiques such as metal tables, antique garden statuary, French furniture of the '30s, hotel silver, and decorative accessories.

Passiflora. 54 Coryell Street. (609)397-1010. "Funk for the soul" is the philosophy for this garden and home store. Passiflora has great-looking pots, soaps, candles, antiques, and whimsical items, some of which spill onto the sidewalk outside. They always have cut flowers on hand and, in summer, some wonderful wild bouquets.

Jack's Furniture and Antiques. 56 Coryell Street. (609)397-2632. A nice selection of old pieces, from the 18th to the 20th centuries. Gorgeous antique mirrors.

Fran Jay Antiques. 10 Church Street. (609)397-1571. Get your Fiestaware, Russell Wright, and Depression glass here. They also carry old toys and other collectibles. Huge selection.

Broadmoor Antiques. 6 North Union Street. (609)397-8802. Ten dealers stock this group shop with taste and class. Merchandise moves in and out fast. Some exquisite decorator items.

The Orchard Hill Collection. 22 North Union Street. (609)397-1188. These folks import Dutch colonial furniture from Asia and it is magnificent, especially the Anglo-Raj pieces. Goes well with antique or contemporary furnishings. Prices are very reasonable for the size of the pieces.

Goldsmiths. 26 North Union Street. (609)397-4590. The fine work of Cynthia Reed and Roger Thompson and other contemporary jewelry designers is shown in this handsome gallery. Sit down with these two designers and have something special made up from the jewelry pieces you no longer wear. Or select something new. They do repairs, too.

The People's Store and The Gallery. 28 North Union Street (two large group antique shops). **The People's Store,** (609)397-9808, has 40 dealers on the street level and basement. **The Gallery,** (609)397-2121, occupies the second floor. Both carry a wide range of items, including some nice paintings, Bakelite jewelry, rugs, and old posters. When you want furniture, look here first.

In fact, look at everything!

A Mano Gallery. 36 North Union Street. (609)397-0063. Contemporary crafts of the finest quality. The glass is particularly interesting. There are stunning wood tables and Marc Coan pottery.

Garden House Antiques. 39 North Union Street. (609)397-9797. Wonderfully decorative items for the home, including extraordinary light fixtures, antique textiles, garden furniture, and silver. The proprietors are engaging.

The Five & Dime. 40 North Union Street. (609)397-4957. Howdy Doody, Superman memorabilia, toys, old Tonka trucks, original Barbies, and other collectibles that appeal to the "boomer" crowd are the stars of this pricey emporium. There are treasures from the '40s, '50s, and '60s everywhere you look.

Phoenix Books. 49 North Union Street. (609)397-4960. For the best used, rare, and out-of-print books, visit Phoenix, practically a Lambertville institution. Browse leisurely in the stacks. You'll love looking through the old LP's and 331/3 records.

Meld. 53 North Union Street. (609)397-8487. Wonderful things from the '50s and '60s, assembled with great whimsy. The choice for anyone interested in barware, martini glasses, or mint julep sets. This store has some super hostess gifts for under $10.

Reinboth and Company. 121 North Union Street (at Delaware). (609)397-2216. This eclectic shop moved recently from a center of town location to a spacious Victorian house. Really a lifestyle more than a store, Reinboth carries natural linens and bedding, lush upholstered furniture, lighting, earthenware pots, candles, and fabulous scents.

Olde English Pine. 202 North Union Street, at Elm Street. (609)397-4978. Armoires, tables, chests, and cocktail tables, all imported from England. Huge selection.

Perrault-Rago Gallery. 17 South Main Street. **(609)397-1802.** The Arts and Crafts movement at the turn of the last century was slow to catch on with contemporary collectors, but now it is going like gangbusters, and this gallery made the market. Simply breathtaking examples of art pottery, glass, tiles, and furniture like Stickley and Mission. A good selection of books about the period, too.

Center City Antiques. 11 Kline's Court. **(609)397-9886.** Group shop filled with chairs, porcelains, lamps, and decorator items. Mostly 19th and 20th century items.

 EATS and TASTY TAKEOUT

Church Street Bistro. 11/2 Church Street. **(609)397-4383.** During the warmer months, open for lunch Wednesday through Sunday. This rustic restaurant is hidden down an alley behind Mitchell's Tavern. Contemporary American cuisine with a French twist. Lovely garden for dining alfresco.

Lambertville Station. 11 Bridge Street. **(609)397-8300.** This is a Victorian-era train station restored to perfection. American foods and lots of space for larger parties. The glass-enclosed dining area that looks out on the Delaware & Raritan Canal is lovely. Lunch and dinner daily. Sunday brunch is particularly nice.

Poets. 49 North Main Street. **(609)397-5990.** Cheesesteaks here are as good as in Philadelphia, and their chicken wings with the requisite accompaniments are legend. Plenty of sandwiches and daily specials. Spacious, good for families.

Homestead Farm Market. 262 North Main Street. **(609)397-8285.** The best locally grown produce, flowers, jams, and baked goods. As the weather warms, the owners bring in a wide-ranging selection of perennials at reasonable prices.

MANASQUAN, POINT PLEASANT, and BAY HEAD

New Jersey is blessed because its best seashore areas are only a little more than an hour from the state's more populated areas. Manasquan and Point Pleasant, two of the more delightful, old-fashioned shore communities located just off the Garden State Parkway, are accessible, family friendly, and filled with shopping opportunities —rain or shine, summer or winter. In Manasquan, there is a factory outlet shopping mall with a small lunch counter and 23 outlets, which advertise 30 to 70 percent off retail prices. The region has scads of lunch and dinner places, many serving fresh-caught seafood. Bay Head is on the Intracoastal Waterway which goes all the way from New Jersey to Florida. Yachting is what chic Bay Head-ers do best, and that and other upscale pastimes are reflected in the town's many shops.

Directions: *For Manasquan, take exit 98* on the Garden State Parkway and head south on Route 34. Go through Allaire traffic circle. Look for the jughandle exit that says Sea Girt-Manasquan on the right. Take that exit and you'll be on Atlantic Avenue. Go about 1 1/2 miles to the Circle Factory Outlets on the right just before the Route 35 circle. To hit Manasquan proper, stay on Atlantic Avenue. After the Route 35 circle, make a right onto Main Street. To get to the beach, head east on Main Street, which becomes East Main Street, and follow it all the way to First Avenue.

To Point Pleasant from Manasquan, turn right on

First Avenue from East Main Street, then turn right again on Brielle Road to Route 71. Make a left on Route 71, then turn left again on Route 35. Broadway and Arnold Avenue are the principal roads that lead from Route 35 east to Point Pleasant Beach. Most of the shopping is along these two streets and Ocean Avenue, Point Pleasant's shore road.

Bay Head and Mantoloking are on Route 35 heading south from Point Pleasant. Turn right on Bridge Avenue to hit the commercial center of Bay Head.

Strategies: Depending on the weather, hit the Manasquan outlets early, then beach it. Or do Point Pleasant Beach and hit the outlets on your way home. If it's sweater weather, go fishing on a party boat or take a sightseeing cruise on the River Belle, both out of Point Pleasant. This town has lots of antique shops – as does Brielle. Bay Head oozes with gorgeous oceanfront homes, so cruise the shore road and then shop. On a summer evening after shopping, it's fun to stroll the Point Pleasant boardwalk with its arcades, find a nice spot to have supper, then take the beach chairs to an outdoor concert at Jenkinson's Inlet Beach on Broadway and Ocean Avenue. Jenkinson's usually has fireworks around 9 p.m. Thursdays in season. Catch a glimpse of Monmouth County's rich history at Historic Allaire Village on Route 524 in Wall Township, (732)938-3311. This was the site of the Howell iron works and a busy industrial center in the 1830s. Today there is a living history museum on the premises, with costumed volunteers doing the interpretations. The gift shop is open daily in the summer, weekends from March to October. There are militia musters, Civil War encampments, flea markets, and fairs on weekends in warmer weather.

 **BEST SHOPPING**

MANASQUAN

Bass Shoe Outlet. 1407 West Atlantic Avenue (at Circle Factory Outlets). (732)528-8117. All the Weejuns, moccasins, and other casual shoes Bass is famous for. The outlet also carries super handbags and carry-alls in attractive designs, backpacks, and even canvas bags for carrying garden tools. Lots of gifts, wallets, and socks.

Famous Brands Housewares. 1407 West Atlantic Avenue (at Circle Factory Outlets). (732)528-0094. Part of the Lechters family, this outlet has most of the cooking gadgets and equipment you'd find in a regular Lechters. However, it carries refurbished coffeemakers from Krups, irons from Rowenta, and appliances from other top manufacturers at truly unbelievable prices. These refurbished pieces are not used. They simply have been damaged in the shipping to retail outlets and returned to the factory, which cleans them up and sends them here.

Geoffrey Beene. 1407 West Atlantic Avenue (at Circle Factory Outlets). (732)528-7210. Well-designed men's sport clothes. New to the store is Beene ladies' wear, and it's truly good-looking the way Geoffrey Beene clothes used to be in the '50s and '60s. Tops and shorts for golf are especially nice.

Jones New York Factory Store, Jones New York Sport, and Jones New York Country. 1407 West Atlantic Avenue (at Circle Factory Outlets). (732)528-5331. See Flemington entry for a description.

Mikasa Factory Store. 1407 West Atlantic Avenue (at Circle Factory Outlets). (732)223-0340. See Secaucus entry for a description.

Nautica Factory Store. 1407 West Atlantic Avenue (at Circle Factory Outlets). (732)528-

1662. See Flemington entry for a description.

Oshkosh B'Gosh. 1407 West Atlantic Avenue (at Circle Factory Outlets). (732)223-8122. Oodles of well-made children's clothes, from infant to youth. All the jeans, overalls, and cotton tees that have made this manufacturer a household word.

Tommy Hilfiger. 1407 West Atlantic Avenue (at Circle Factory Outlets). (732)223-6888. See Flemington entry for a description.

Chantilly Wicker. 108 Main Street. (732)223-1434. A store that is just the ticket for "down the shore." Beautiful wicker furniture and decorative items. Picture frames, pillows, gifts.

Carriage House Antique Center. 140 Main Street. (732) 528-6772. The center houses the goods of 20 dealers. There is a lot of glass and china, some dolls, quilts, art, and silver. The best pieces are wicker. They would look great on an oceanfront porch.

Rare Cargo. 175 Main Street. (732)223-5709. A rather trendy clothing store for women, with creative clothes that go with today's lifestyles. Some of the designers they carry are Cooperative and CK, the moderate Calvin Klein brand. Teenagers and younger women will love it.

Victoria Fine Furniture. 35 Broad Street. (732)223-6788. Fine furniture, suitable for shore or suburban living, coupled with beautiful accessories and gifts.

 EATS and TASTY TAKEOUT

Center Food Market. 113 Main Street. (732)223-4556. The interior is like an old-fashioned general store, except the shelves are stocked with gourmet items and Pops never offered a pesto sandwich with sun-dried tomatoes on an Italian roll. The sandwiches are enormous — perfect for picnic baskets. There are daily specials and soups, cole slaw, cold pastas, and salads by the pound. Ample espressos, cappuccinos, and lattes.

Leggett's Sand Bar. 217 First Avenue. (732)223-3951. Across from the beach. Good food and thirst-quenching drinks.

T.J.'s Corner Store. Ocean Avenue and First Avenue. (732)223-5765. Open breakfast and lunch. Right across from the beach. A great local favorite.

Hinck Turkey Farm. 414 Atlantic Avenue (across from Circle Factory Outlets). (732)223-5622. Fresh-cooked turkey to take out, absolutely the highest quality. Platters, trimmings, turkeys sliced and put back on frame. They also sell breads, pies, cakes, cookies, and fruit tarts.

 **BEST SHOPPING**

POINT PLEASANT

Point Pleasant Antique Emporium. Bay and Trenton Avenues. 1-800-322-8002 or (732)892-2222. This place is huge, with 90 dealers offering exceptional quality clocks, folk art, quilts, porcelains, and you name it. This is one of the largest antique centers in New Jersey. A fun place to visit for neophytes or buffs.

The Time Machine. 516 Arnold Avenue. (732)295-9695. Vintage music, '50s and '60s TV memorabilia, toys, good collectibles.

The Snow Goose. 641 Arnold Avenue. (732)892-6929. Eclectic selection of antiques in an antique setting.

Gold Fever...Catch It. 700 Arnold Avenue (at Bay Avenue). (732)892-3535. A nice selection of wedding bands and engagement rings plus estate jewelry and gifts. You'll find pre-owned and vintage watches here by makers such as Rolex.

Wally's Follies. 718 Arnold Avenue. (732)899-1840. This is the place to come for wicker. If your own wicker needs repair, this shop is one of the few places in New Jersey that does it right. They also do caning, rushing, bamboo repairs, and faux finishing.

Willingers Annex. 626 Ocean Road. (732)892-2217. A group shop of 20 dealers. Selections of the finest antiques from estates and big old shore homes.

Shore Antique Center. 300 Richmond Avenue (at Route 35 South). (732)295-5771. About 30 dealers show their wares here. Everything from art glass, steins, and silver to furniture for a summer house. Huge selection.

EATS and TASTY TAKEOUT

Europa South. Route 35 and Arnold Avenue. (732)295-1500. Portuguese and Spanish cuisines. Paellas, pollo, and mariscadas. Unique at the shore. Open for lunch and dinner seven days a week.

Natural Buffet. 608 Ocean Avenue. (732)295-4548. All you can eat and the food is natural, very fresh. Open seven days, 6 a.m. to 9 p.m. The crowd at dinner is quite large, so go early.

Peter Skokos Drive-in. 25 Broadway. (732)892-3420. When you're hot and need respite from the beach but don't want to walk far, this is the place. Good burgers.

BEST SHOPPING

BAY HEAD

Fables of Bay Head. 410 Main Avenue. (732)899-3633. This is a terrific shop near the beach, very appealing, with antique folk art, furniture, and gifts. When you feel the need for ice cream, stop in for a cone.

The Lathrop Tree. 534 Lake Avenue. (732)295-

8282. Casual cotton sport clothing for ladies and kids, many beautifully screen-printed.

Mark, Fore & Strike. 68 Bridge Avenue. (732)892-6721. Part of a chain of preppy clothing stores, headquartered in Florida and located in and around East Coast resort communities, this shop carries cotton shirts, shorts, and slacks for men and women. The cotton sweaters are wonderful. Large Nautica selection.

Dee's Antiques and Collectibles. 70 Bridge Avenue (in Shoppers Wharf). (732)899-8400. Genteel selection of china, glassware, and smalls.

Rhody's. 70 Bridge Avenue. (732)295-4944. Lovely picture frames, clothing, and household gifts in colors that would fit into a primary or vacation home.

The WASP. 76 Bridge Avenue. (732)899-9277. Tees and sweatshirts imprinted with Bay Head or Mantoloking logos, plus a selection of bright-colored Lilly Pulitzer florals. Gifts for boaters, tennis players, and other sport-minded individuals. **The Bee** next door has more contemporary clothing.

Bay Head Outfitters. 92 Bridge Avenue. (732)892-8008. Handsome-looking shop for active people, especially fishing enthusiasts. Ladies' and men's sport clothes, well-designed tees and sweatshirts bearing the shop's own logo, men's bathing suits, gifts, artwork, tackle. Carries the Orvis line.

 EATS and TASTY TAKEOUT

CJ's Ice Cream and Yogurt. Bridge Avenue and Bay Avenue. (732)899-0123. Homemade ice cream and frozen yogurts that are truly delicious. Stop in when you are dragging.

The Grenville Hotel and Restaurant. 345 Main Avenue. (732)892-3100. Lunch, dinner, and brunch on Sunday couldn't be more perfect than in this Victorian near the sea. Striped awnings, wicker, and beautiful appointments. Cuisine is creative American.

WORTH a DETOUR
BRIELLE

Directions: From Manasquan, head south on Route 71 into Brielle, the adjoining community.

Brielle Galleries. 707 Union Avenue (Route 71). (732)528-8400. This is where you will see one of the largest selections of china, sterling, crystal, and dining accessories in New Jersey. But there are also gifts, stationery and invitations, wallets, kitchenware, and chocolates. Shoppers include prospective brides and their mothers.

ALONG ROUTE 9, MATAWAN to FREEHOLD

This was farming country once, but now the proliferation of malls and strip shopping centers has made the area a shopper's paradise. Some of the smaller stores can be marginal and may close after a few months, but new ones always seem to open to take their places. The granddaddy of bargain shopping is also located here, Englishtown Auction Sales, which bills itself as New Jersey's premiere open-air market. If you've never spent a spring or summer Saturday at Englishtown, you have been depriving yourself of a fun-filled recreational shopping experience.

Directions: To start at Matawan, take the Garden State Parkway south through the Driscoll Bridge toll and get in the local lanes. Get off almost immediately at Route 9 South and go about three miles to Route 34 South (bear to the left). A mile up on the left is the Market Place and Market Place II. Return to Route 9 the same way you came or continue south on Route 34 to Route 516. Go toward Old Bridge on Route 516 and you will hit Route 9 further down.

To get to Englishtown market, head south on Route 9 to Gordons Corner Road and make a right. At the traffic light at the junction of Gordons Corner Road and Route 527, turn left onto Route 527 and go one mile to the market. If you want to visit Englishtown direct from the New Jersey Turnpike, get off at Exit 9 (New Brunswick) and head south on Route 18. Go through East Brunswick and continue on past Spotswood at which point you'll see Route 527 on your right. Take it all the way down to Englishtown. The market will be on your left.

Strategies: There may be superhumans who can shop this region in one day, but I recommend doing it in two. Englishtown is open Saturdays and Sundays only. Get up early and hit the market at 8 a.m. Have breakfast in one of the excellent restaurants on site, then head to the stalls. For Route 9 area shops, start at the Market Place at Matawan, then go south to Freehold and Howell beyond.

For a change of pace, you can walk in the footsteps of history at Monmouth Battlefield State Park, Business Route 33 West in Manalapan, 1 1/2 miles from Route 9, (732)462-9616. This is where heroine Molly Pitcher made her mark. A small museum has exhibits and audio-visual displays. Visit the picnic area and small playground. One weekend a year, usually in June, there is a two-day encampment in which men and women reenact the Battle of Monmouth. Only then is there a small admission charge.

One of New Jersey's great horseracing venues is the Freehold Raceway, located at Routes 9 and 33 in Freehold, just off the Freehold Circle, (732)462-3800. The raceway is open from mid-

August to Memorial Day and alternates trotters and pacers. Racing is at 1 p.m. in fall and spring, 12:30 p.m. in the winter months. The clubhouse has a restaurant and in the grandstand are a cafeteria and several food concessions.

 **BEST SHOPPING**

MATAWAN

Bare Necessities. Route 34 and Disbrow Road (in the Matawan Marketplace). (732)583-3878. Huge selection of bras, underpants, and nighties from the most popular manufacturers. Prices are about 20 percent lower than you'd find elsewhere. Large selection of bras and girdles for the full-figured woman. One of the few places to find longline bras that extend below the waist. Vanity Fair, Bali, and Olga undergarments, as well as cute Jones New York cotton nightgowns.

Calico Corners. Route 34 and Disbrow Road (in the Matawan Marketplace). (732)583-5223. See East Hanover entry under Morristown for description.

Carter's Childrenswear Factory Outlet. Route 34 and Disbrow Road (in the Matawan Marketplace). (732)583-8391. Here's where you come for the basics – the stretchies, underpants, undershirts, and socks that every infant and toddler seems to go through in great numbers. Some very attractive playsets.

L'Eggs-Hanes-Bali Factory Outlet. Route 34 and Disbrow Road (in the Matawan Marketplace). (732)583-6183. Good discounts on top manufacturer undergarments and hosiery. Looking for the Wonderbra? They have lots of styles here.

Susan Greene Handbags, Jewelry & Luggage. Route 34 and Disbrow Road (in the Matawan Marketplace). (732)583-3696. Nicely made leather bags at discount prices, some from

Italy and South America. Lots of backpacks suitable for school or casual wear. There is an incredible selection of luggage from Samsonite, Verdi, and Lark, including many with wheels and retractable handles for easy pulling.

Van Heusen Direct. **Route 34 and Disbrow Road (in the Matawan Marketplace). (732)566-2434.** This discount house features moderately priced dress shirts for men, starting with a 15 neck and going up to large sizes. Button-down and spread collar. Also ties and belts plus casual sportswear for men and women.

EATS and TASTY TAKEOUT

Big Ed's Barbecue. **174 Route 34 (on the Matawan-Old Bridge line). (732)583-2626.** Ribs the way they're served in Texas or North Carolina – big, sloppy, and delicious.

BEST SHOPPING
ENGLISHTOWN

Englishtown Auction Sales. **90 Wilson Avenue (Route 527). (732)446-9644.** Open every Saturday from 7 a.m. to 4 p.m., every Sunday from 9 a.m. to 4 p.m. Also open Good Friday, Labor Day, the day after Thanksgiving, and the five days prior to Christmas from 9 a.m. to 4 p.m. More than 300 indoor shops and restaurants plus hundreds of outdoor vendors on this 40-acre property.

The first time you go, expect to be overwhelmed because there are indoor and outdoor vendors and you may not be able to develop a strategy for seeing them all. The second time around, you'll learn how to handle this monster of a market. The outdoor vendors are situated along dusty paths known as "streets." Fifth Avenue runs along the left side of the principal market and Times Square-42nd Street runs on the right. Cross streets are Broadway, Orchard, and Lexington. There are smaller cross streets such as Bowery, Canal, Mott, and Wall located in the market annex, which is located to the left of Fifth Avenue. Sesame Street and Lois Lane are among the more clever names here.

The more established vendors are in steel-frame buildings that are color-coded, so when you hear an announcement over the loudspeaker that there is a special sale in the Red Building, you'll know where to head.

Best buys include linens and towels such as high-quality bathsheets for $5, real down pillows, perfumes (half what you'd pay in a department store), sneakers from Nike and Reebok, luggage, lingerie from Victoria's Secret and other top retailers, crafts, fresh produce, and even computers. Naturally, there are dozens of tee shirt booths, but some vendors carry brands such as Nautica and Tommy Hilfiger. Along Lexington Avenue is a vendor selling nice Gap jeans. Susan Greene, a shop with one outlet at the Marketplace in Matawan, has another shop in the Brown Building, Booths 46-48, where there are great bargains on handbags. Browsers at the Englishtown Market will see costly leather coats, 14 karat gold jewelry, books, pet supplies, gift wrappings, and housewares. But look out, because there is a lot of just plain junk, too.

Park in the $2 lot across from the entrance for best ingress and egress. Go early because many vendors pack up to leave before closing time, especially in the heat of a summer afternoon.

 EATS and TASTY TAKEOUT

Sushi Hut. Brown Building, Booth 44. Andy and Kenny Yeh dispense sushi with cooked seafood such as shrimp, scallops, and soft-shelled crabs.

Simply superb. Also great chicken wings.

Gourmet Hotdog Stand. At the back of the market where Fifth Avenue and Lexington Avenue come together. This stand serves the fine Isaac Gellis brand of garlicky Kosher hot dogs with kraut and all the trimmings. You can't eat just one.

Dudley's Pretzels. Red Building. This stand dishes up really huge pretzels.

 ## BEST SHOPPING

MARLBORO

Shelly's Touch. 204 Route 9 North (just before Marlboro Plaza). (732)536-6556. The owner has simply beautiful taste in ladies' clothes. Here is where you'd find a fancy beaded dress for a Bar Mitzvah or wedding. Wide selection. Also some everyday wear, but not really suitable for work. About a 20 percent discount.

Smith Bros. 126 Route 9 North (in Marlboro Plaza). (732)972-1130. Excellent selection of funky clothes for teens and college women. Good-looking fashions at prices that will allow shoppers to buy two or three outfits instead of one.

 ## EATS and TASTY TAKEOUT

Kyoto. 420 Route 9 North (just before Union Hill Road and the new Shop-Rite Shopping Center). (732)972-2225. A Japanese restaurant with exceptional sushi. Lunch and dinner.

 ## BEST SHOPPING

MANALAPAN

Shoes by Wayne Stevens. 309 Route 9 South (in Alexander Plaza). (732)780-2521. Excellent selection of designer shoes and handbags.

Rosanne's of Brooklyn. 345 Route 9 South (in the Design Center). (732)866-8870. The ladies' clothing in this spacious shop is well-selected, tailored, and appropriate for the office or business evenings. Moderate prices.

Kas II. 357 Route 9 South (in the Design Shopping Center). (732)866-9292. This is one of the best stores for dance and hot-looking aerobics wear. They carry Capezio shoes and accessories, Baryshnikov clothing, Danskin, Freed, Mirella, and Duck Crossing, to name just a few of the brands. Super service.

Harmon Discount. 357 Route 9 South (in the Towne Pointe Shopping Center). (732)972-0663. Super buys on make-up, expensive shampoos and conditioners like KeriSilk, Aveda, and Hi-Pro-Pac, as well as sundries.

Jasper Shoes. 357 Route 9 South (in the Towne Pointe Shopping Center). (732)972-2323. Very fashionable imported shoes, always ahead of the styles.

Lola's. 357 Route 9 South (in the Towne Pointe Shopping Center). (732)577-0066. Fine avant garde clothing for infants and children. Lots of leopard and fake leather! In addition to the wild outfits, some really frilly, feminine party dresses for teens and pre-teens, suitable for Bar and Bat Mitzvahs.

Rudi's Pottery Silver China & Gifts. 357 Route 9 South (in the Towne Pointe Shopping Center). 1-800-836-4438. See Paramus entry for a description.

The Right Angle Gallery. 100 Route 9 North (in the Galleria Shopping Center). (732)431-5222. Exquisite American crafts, jewelry, framing, and pottery that can be inscribed for the celebrations of one's life.

Marty's Shoe Outlet. 302 Route 9 North (in Exclusive Plaza). (732)972-8445. Shoes to fit the whole family, from flats for her to sneakers for your teen. Some excellent buys from Westies,

Cobbies, and Keds in casual shoes and Italian designers for dress.

 EATS and TASTY TAKEOUT

Chu's Sweets and Bakery. 100 Route 9 North (in the Galleria Shopping Center). (732)845-0888. For aficionados of Chinese sweets. Bao rolls filled with bean paste and lots of new and different taste sensations. Go ahead and try.

Jesse & David's Kosher Experience. 357 Route 9 South (in Towne Pointe Shopping Center). (732)972-7755. Giant sandwiches of corned beef, pastrami, turkey, brisket, and meat loaf in every combination or permutation. Everything made fresh on premises. Take-out counter has kasha and bow ties, roasted potatoes, and a cabbage stuffed with chicken that is out of this world.

 BEST SHOPPING

FREEHOLD

Freehold Raceway Mall. 3710 Route 9. (732)577-1144. About three years ago, super department store shopping came to Freehold when this mall went up. **Lord & Taylor, Nordstrom's, Sears,** and **Penney's** are the anchor stores. Macy's will be coming in fall 1998. The other stores in the mall are pretty typical of the ones found in malls like Bridgewater Commons — The Gap, Banana Republic, etc. Elsewhere on the mall grounds, which are vast, are a **Sam's Club** discount warehouse, **Builders Square, Toys 'R Us,** a **Marshalls** (we adore their sheets, towels, and kids' clothes), and a **Bob's Store.**

EATS and **TASTY TAKEOUT**

Jersey Freeze. At the Freehold Circle on Route 9. (732)946-8163. Homemade ice cream in a myriad of flavors. Jersey Freeze has been in business nearly half a century and it's a real institution in this area. You may be eating non-fat frozen yogurt, but you'll never know it's not ice cream. It's that good! An adjoining restaurant has burgers, grilled cheese, and salads.

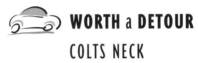 **WORTH** a **DETOUR**

COLTS NECK

Directions: *From Freehold,* take Route 537 (Colt's Neck Road) to Route 34 and turn right.

Delicious Orchards. 36 Route 34. (732)462-1989. The most mouth-watering produce alongside home-baked fruit pies, breads, pastries, flowers, annuals, and cider. Delicious Orchards is an institution in this part of New Jersey, and at Thanksgiving, thousands come to buy their pies at this very upscale fruit and vegetable stand. Outside, grab a cart; you'll need it. In summer, pick your own raspberries (red and black) at the Berry Farm, which is adjacent to this sprawling market.

The Birds and the Beads. 41 Route 34 South. (732)780-1926. This tiny shop is well stocked with semiprecious beads for jewelry-making.

Liguori and Hunt Ltd. 41 Route 34 South. (732)462-4014. Throughout this shop are examples of fine kitchenware and table settings. It is very inviting.

Folio Art Glass. 73 Route 34 South. (732)431-0044. This shop sells beautiful pieces that would be suitable for wedding gifts.

EAST BRUNSWICK

Directions: From Marlboro, follow Route 18 North approximately 7 miles (past the Milltown Road exit).

Route 18 Market. 290 Route 18 North. (732)254-5082. An indoor flea market open Friday to Sunday only, with evening hours on Fridays and Saturdays. Lots of on-site parking. This is the kind of market that used to be prevalent throughout New Jersey but which has succumbed in recent years to upscale redevelopment. Look for a fun mix of casual clothing for adults and children, toys, hair ornaments, comic books, collectibles, antiques, jewelry, bulk candy and nuts, and junk foods. Prices are excellent.

PRINCETON

Princeton is a great university town, Central New Jersey's cultural oasis, and a bastion of colonial heritage, but it is also home to some unusual retail shops. Stores catering to the Princeton faculty and highbrow community are sophisticated while shops and eateries for students are distinctly preppy. Recently, the gentrification of Palmer Square at Nassau Street, the town's prime retail thoroughfare, has caused some of the longtime emporia across from the university to move to back streets or go out of business altogether. In their places are the chain stores such as the Gap, Ann Taylor, and Burger King. Outside Princeton on Route 1, small-scale shopping malls augment the Nassau Street experience.

Directions: _From Northern Jersey,_ take the New Jersey Turnpike to Exit 8A. Take Route 32 toward

Princeton. Turn left on Route 130 and right on Cranbury-Plainsboro-Princeton Road to Route 1. Turn left onto Route 1 and take either Harrison Street or Washington Road into the Nassau Street shopping district.

From Northern and Central Jersey, take Route 287 South to the Route 202-206 South exit. At the Somerville Circle, take Route 206 South and go 15 miles to Princeton. At the light at Nassau Street, turn left to the shopping district.

Strategies: Parking can be difficult in the borough as shoppers, business people, and students and their visitors all compete for the same spaces. All-day parkers should look for the inexpensive Palmer Square deck off Hulfish Street or the metered lots behind Witherspoon. For shorter shopping trips, one can usually find metered spaces on Palmer Square West, the street adjacent to the Nassau Inn, or occasionally on Chambers Street off Nassau Street. Stores have been staying open Thursday and Friday nights, but check before you come. Most stay open Sunday afternoons, as well.

 **BEST SHOPPING**

Go For Baroque. 20 Nassau Street. (609)497-3500. From "message" stones and shaving razors with personality to delicate, handblown-glass salt and peppers, this small corner store is filled with a changing selection of very sophisticated personal gifts and home accessories selected by the shop's three owners on their travels here and abroad. Many items have a touch of whimsy. This is a great place to purchase a truly unique present for that special person or occasion.

April Cornell. 51 Palmer Square West. (609)921-3559. This shop is part of a chain that establishes beachheads in upscale college towns and tourist areas and it seems to fit Palmer Square like a glove. Natural fabric clothing that appeals to a younger crowd in addition to terrific-looking tablecloths, placemats, bedspreads, and duvets in hand-blocked prints from India. This is the middle class's Pierre Deux.

Sweet Kendall. 67 Palmer Square West. (609)683-8393. One of the town's choicest shops for women. Flax, PA, and other fine cottons in casual and professional wear are abundant during the warmer months. Winter stock-in-trade are the chenille sweaters and floaty dressy dresses. Hats, gloves, and delicate footwear complement the clothing line. Sweet Kendall is widely known for its jewelry of the '30s and '40s.

Matteo & Co. 69 Palmer Square West. (609)430-1400. Recently opened by Tamera Matteo, this delightful shop carries unusual items for the home, including exquisite bed linens from Angel Zimick. In addition to the thick bathroom towels and floral soaps Matteo stocks, there are floppy sofas, antique refinished cupboards, and handmade reed baby baskets with gingham bumpers. Most of the sheets are in queen, but anything can be ordered.

Simon Pearce. 72 Palmer Square West. (609)279-0444. It used to be Steuben, then Baccarat, but now everyone wants Simon Pearce glassware. Made in Vermont, its clean lines and verve are infectious. Expensive, but look for seconds in glassware, salad bowls, vases, and lamps that could shave 30 to 40 percent off the retail price. Quite a large selection of seconds.

Steilmann. 15 Hulfish Street. (609)683-5650. Steilmann (pronounced style-man) is a German manufacturer of rather tailored women's clothing, sort of a junior Escada. The store stocks the Steilmann line of coats, blazers, and skirts in conservative blacks and navys as well in the luscious limes and over-the-top oranges. The designer's custom KS line is also available. After the holidays, there are wonderful sales on coats.

Waverly Home. One Palmer Square. (609)683-0505. When H. Gross & Co., outfitters to generations of Princeton men and women, moved to 51 Hulfish Street, in came Waverly Home. Now ensconced at Princeton's most prestigious shopping address, the two-level store glitters with upholstered furniture and fabrics from Waverly and Schumacher & Co., of which Waverly is a division. Also decorative and seasonal items, all very well put together.

J. McLaughlin. 17 Witherspoon Street. **(609)497-9717.** Rich-looking, preppy clothing for college-age men and women and those 20- and 30-somethings out in the work force. Handsome sports jackets for the guys; blazers and skirts for the women. Casual but elegant is the emphasis here. The store also has some unique sweaters for men and women. Nice, helpful staff.

A Little Taste of Cuba. 70 Witherspoon Street. **(609)683-8988.** I love the aromas awaft in this paneled cigar parlor, designed and run by master tobacconist Jorge L. Armenteros. The walk-in humidor is behind glass, mysterious and appealing. On the shelves are hand-rolled cigars with Cuban lineage, if not manufacture, priced by the piece or the dozen. Cigar accessories abound, such as portable humidors, leather cigar cases, and lots of reading material. There are a few lounge chairs for smokers.

Graves Design Studio Store. 338 Nassau Street (at Harrison). **(609)497-6878.** A healthy walk north on Nassau Street from the downtown shopping district, this small, precious space in a once-private residence across from architect Michael Graves' office houses home furnishings and accessories of his design. Ring the doorbell. Many pieces are manufactured in Italy, from the whistling bird and ferris teakettles made by Alessi to rotund clocks in rare woods, picture frames, frosted glass bath accessories, and fine china. The shop closes rather early on weekdays, around 4 p.m., but weekend hours are longer.

 **EATS and TASTY TAKEOUT**

Halo Pub. **9 Hulfish Street. (609)921-1710.** For a quick pick-me-up, stop into Halo Pub at the foot of Palmer Square for premium, Trenton-made ice cream in a zillion gourmet flavors to rival Ben and Jerry's. The shop, charmingly decorated with "cow" memorabilia and antique ice cream scoops, also serves coffee beverages. Best prices in town on ice cream and coffee.

Teresa's Pizzetta Caffe. **21 Palmer Square East. (609)921-1974.** Wood-burning ovens create the most delicate of pizzas in this attractive trattoria and wine bar. Choose from a variety of toppings. The pastas are light and the salads fresh.

Triumph Brewing Company. **138 Nassau Street. (609)924-7855.** The entrance may be unprepossessing, but one eventually emerges from a long corridor to a trendy two-level restaurant and brew pub that's often mobbed – go early or late. Sandwiches are the best bet, some served on delicious focaccia or sourdough toast. Knockwursts go well with the outstanding beers and ales.

Chez Alice. **254 Nassau Street (on the way to the Graves Design Studio Store). (609)921-6707.** Fine French patisserie and gourmet entrees and salads all prepared on the premises by proprietor Alice de Tiberge. If you can't wait until you get home, freshly brewed coffee is available to wash down one of the irresistible treats.

Nassau Street Seafood Co. **256 Nassau Street (on the way to the Graves Design Studio Store). (609)921-0620.** The place in town for impeccably fresh fish and perfect produce. After a full day of shopping, take home some of the excellent prepared foods. There are hearth-baked breads and Terhune's farm-baked pies to round out the meal and colorful bunches of flowers to brighten the table.

 **WORTH a DETOUR**

HIGHTSTOWN

Directions: *From Princeton,* take Route 571 (Washington Road) south to Route 130 in West Windsor. Turn right onto Route 130 South and, at the second traffic light, turn right onto Hickory Corner Road.

Lee Turkey Farm. 201 Hickory Corner Road. **(609)448-0629.** At Thanksgiving and all year, Lee's has the very best in premium quality, corn-fed turkeys. A supermarket turkey tastes like cardboard after this. Home-grown fruits and vegetables such as raspberries, eggplant, pears, and melons, available at the market or pick-your-own. Take the kids on hayrides in the fall. A hotline tells what the farm is picking day by day in good weather.

HOPEWELL

A quaint country town with shady streets to wander full of antique shops.

Directions: *From Princeton,* take Nassau Street south to the Elm Road traffic light. Turn right onto Elm and go straight, staying on Elm (it becomes The Great Road) out to Cherry Valley Road. Make a left onto Cherry Valley Road and turn right on Route 569 to get into Hopewell.

Tomato Factory Antique Center. 2 Somerset Street (parallel to Broad Street at the end of Hamilton Avenue). **(609)466-9833.** The center encompasses 15,000 square feet of country and formal antiques, furniture, lamps, toys, dolls, jewelry, and Fiestaware. There are goodies stuffed into every nook and cranny of this former manufacturing plant. Open every day. Also check out **Ninotchka** at 35 West Broad Street, **(609)466-0556,** for interesting china and smalls, and **High Button Shoe,** 2 Bank Place (off Blackwell Avenue), **(609)466-9807.**

EATS and TASTY TAKEOUT

Soupe du Jour. 10 East Broad Street (parking and entrance on Blackwell Avenue). (609)466-3777. The soups of this establishment really hit the spot, especially in colder weather. There are all kinds of sandwiches, salads, and accompaniments.

PLAINSBORO

Directions: *From Princeton,* head out on Washington Road to Route 1, then go north 2 miles. For the Forrestal Village/Marriott complex, you will have to take the jughandle back across Route 1.

Princeton Forrestal Village. Route 1 at College Road West (behind the Marriott). (609)799-7400. A conglomeration of factory outlets, this mall seems to have a steady stream of retail occupants going in and out of business. More or less a fixture is the ***WestPoint Pepperell Mill Store*** at 101 Rockingham Row, (609)987-1150, where one can always get Ralph Lauren linens, either seconds or greatly reduced. The store carries a full complement of Lauren bedding, from dust ruffles to duvet covers. Other good buys are on European white goose down comforters, J.P. Stevens linens, Martex towels, and special occasion items such as tablecloths, votive candle-holders, and tabletop decorations. ***Leather Loft*** at 104 Rockingham Row, (609)734-0650, carries handsome Kenneth Cole briefcases, wallets, and handbags at about 30 percent off retail. ***Dansk*** is here at 120 Main Street, (609)520-0077, and although the store is small for a Dansk outlet, it carries good crystal and glassware, oversize wicker baskets, dinnerware, salad bowls, and gift items. ***Oneida Factory Store,*** (609)951-9550, has good buys in flatware, including the elegant designs that look like formal silver but are really indestructible stainless steel. There are also silverplated serving trays and some terrific baby gifts. **TerraCotta,** a small tile shop located at **124 Stanhope Street, (609)520-0075,** has sales from time to time on individual tiles and some pottery pieces, but it is not a discount store like so many others in Forrestal Village. However, for those considering a tile kitchen, marble bath, or a mosaic porch, it is one of the premiere places to shop in New Jersey. From Thanksgiving through mid-December, the shopping center management promotes its Village Values Card, which entitles the holder to 10 percent off already-discounted prices at participating stores.

ROCKY HILL

Directions: *From Princeton,* take Nassau Street south to the traffic light at Route 206. Turn right onto Route 206 and travel north 4 miles to Route 518. Turn right onto Route 518. It becomes Washington Street in the village.

John Shedd Designs. **200 Washington Street. (609)924-6394.** High-quality pottery and glass from several designers, including John Shedd, make an excellent gift. The seconds are terrific buys! Get on the mailing list for inventory clearance sales.

RED BANK and RED BANK PENINSULA

Between the Navesink and Shrewsbury rivers in Monmouth County, where at almost every turn are views of calm water and where old sea captain's houses host upscale shops, a most pleasurable day can be spent. The centerpiece of this sparkling peninsula is the Borough of Red Bank, which is enjoying a renaissance of late as more and more people discover what Red Bank has the most of – location, location, location. Building restorations are already common on Broad Street and Front Street, the two prime shopping thoroughfares, but in a few years there will be gaslights, coblestone plazas, and clear views to the Navesink. The antique district is chockablock full of shops, tiny and vast, and nearby a dilapidated factory building has been restored and reincarnated as The Galleria, a collection of chic restaurants, shops, and a pool hall. Communities to the south like Fairhaven, Rumson, and Little Silver have long had a kind of magic. In fact, some call them "Hollywood East" for the concentration of celebrities like Bruce Springsteen and Geraldo Rivera, who happens to own a local newspaper.

Directions: To get to Red Bank, take the Garden State Parkway to Exit 109, Red Bank. Go south on Route 520 to the intersection of Route 35. Go left onto Route 35, which becomes Broad Street, Red Bank. To reach West Front Street, go to the end of Broad Street and turn left.

To Fairhaven from Red Bank, take Front Street south and, after it changes its name to River Road, you will be in Fairhaven.

To Little Silver from River Road in Rumson, make a right on Bingham Avenue and then another right onto Rumson Avenue North (Route 520). After 2 miles, veer left onto Church Street to the Little Silver business district.

To Rumson from Red Bank and Fairhaven, continue on River Road to reach Rumson.

Strategies: Red Bank is really a two-park job – park once in the downtown and once in the antique district along West Front Street to see it all. Good parking lots are scattered behind Broad Street. The biggest one is on White Street. Traveling along Broad Street from Route 520, pass Monmouth Street on the left. The next left is White. The lot is in the middle of the block. Visit

Red Bank first, have lunch, and head to the other locations. End with a stop at Sickles Farm.

BEST SHOPPING

RED BANK

Clayton and Magee. 19 Broad Street. **(732)747-2315.** This is one of the most unusual shops you will ever see. Well-tailored men's and boys' clothes, formal and sporty, and a huge display of American crafts that include handblown wineglasses, vases, desk and wall clocks, and whimsical sculptures. Owner Don Magee is a collector who believed that Red Bank needed an outlet for contemporary crafts and he's been proved correct.

Garmany. 105 Broad Street. (732)576-8500. For the fashion-forward gentleman who wears or wants to try Armani, Hugo Boss, Zegna, Iceberg, and other European designers, Garmany is the place to go in this part of New Jersey. Located in the newly renovated Roots building, Garmany is known for helping men put together a look. The shop also carries shoes from Ferragamo, Cole Haan, and Magli.

Tower Hill Antiques & Design. 147 Broad Street. (732)842-5551. A lot of country furniture suitable for a shore cottage, formal furniture, silver, china, and decorative art. Very nice selection. On the second floor is the studio of **Barbara Pivnick,** a quilter. She takes gorgeous fabrics, domestic and imported, and makes quilts and wall-hangings out of them. Call her at (732)219-8996 before coming since she is not always there.

Tea & Vintage. 16 West Front Street. **(732)741-6676.** An unusual and interesting shop that combines a restaurant where traditional English teas are served with a boutique that specializes in well-preserved vintage clothing and jewelry.

Copper Kettle Antiques. 169 West Front Street. (732)741-8583. One of the best antique shops in town, with a wide selection of fine furniture, jewelry, art, and smalls.

Riverbank Antiques & Interiors. 169 West Front Street. (732)842-5400. Approximately 30 dealers in this well-decorated group shop. Some nice iron beds, wicker, mirrors, and small items.

The Antique Center of Red Bank. 226 West Front Street. (732)842-4336. There are 150 dealers in three buildings and their wares run the gamut from fine and fancy to '30s collectibles like refrigerator glass. You will see examples of the Arts and Crafts and Moderne movements, silver, pens, baseball cards and memorabilia, vintage clothing, and folk art. The list of items just goes on and on. Give yourself time to browse because there's a lot to see. Open 7 days. Dealers are there to assist shoppers.

Monmouth Antique Shoppes. 217 West Front Street. (732)842-7377. In the heart of the antique district, this 30-member group shop has everything from Fiestaware to furniture.

Cocoon. 28 Monmouth Street. (732)747-1733. The name of this shop describes best what's inside — clothing, furniture, and home accessories that envelop shoppers in a parallel universe of good design. Owner Roseann Bost opened three years ago, representing the best of women's designers like Flax and No Saint plus bed linens from Area and Hot Knots knitted wear. The handmade futons produced by a women's cooperative from the Midwest are wonderful.

Jay and Bob's Secret Stash. 69 Monmouth Street. (732)758-0508. New comics for the summer camp set and movie merchandise. Lots of collectible cards.

Galleria Gold Company. 2 Bridge Avenue (in The Galleria). (732)747-3337. The real stuff and the marcasite jewelry of Judith Jack.

Down to Basics. 12 Bridge Avenue (in The Galleria). (732)741-6800. It started with down comforters, but then Down to Basics branched out to sheets from Palais Royal and other fine designers, baby quilts, stuffed animals, and gifts, A tasteful, elegant shop.

Homewares Ltd. 40 Bridge Avenue (in The Galleria). (732)530-7100. This store stocks well-designed items for the kitchen, bedroom, and bathroom.

Wild Flower Antiques. 19 North Bridge Avenue. (732)933-7733. This shop just opened in this location after several years in the group shop at Riverbank Antiques. Owner Susan Hough has a marvelous eye for cottage furnishings — charming tables, desks, chairs, and stands in old paint plus English transferware china of the '30s, garden urns, and prints.

Billi. 50 English Plaza. (732)530-8142. Soho-style clothing, trendy and chic. For men and women.

Nana's Doll House Miniatures Shop. 54 English Plaza. (732)842-4411. Little girls, big girls, and even guys get a kick out of Nana's perfectly formed dollhouses and furniture, rugs, and lighting to scale. Everything for the Lilliputian household!

Stems. 32 White Street. (732)219-8888. A flower "studio," rather than a florist shop, Stems offers stunning arrangements of fresh and dried blooms in one-of-a-kind containers. Look for the hand-tinted floral photographs mounted on canvas. They are created by the husband of one of the shop's owners.

 EATS and TASTY TAKEOUT

Broadway Diner. 45 Monmouth Street. (732)224-1234. Trendy, with its neon and hot menu. Red Bank's fun place, 24 hours a day!

Le Bistro. 14 Broad Street. (732)530-5553. Locals in the know dig into this restaurant's exquisite contemporary fare, but many admire the ambiance as well.

Molly Pitcher Inn. 88 Riverside Avenue. (732)747-2500. Red Bank's most venerable spot for lunch. The interior is decorated with gorgeous dark woods and rich fabrics. Fine American fare.

La Perle. 146 Bodman Place (at the Oyster Point Hotel). (732)530-0111. Heaven is a summer lunch on the deck overlooking the Navesink. All the finest seafood specialties in this restaurant that is part of a hotel and marina.

Sant' Arsenio Panificio Artigiano. 52A Monmouth Street. (732)530-8208. If you come to Red Bank for one reason, come for baker Anthony Mangieri's handmade Neopolitan breads and rolls in such creative combinations as wheat with crunchy walnuts and almonds, wheat with olives, or semolina with tangy herbs. He traveled to his family's village in Italy to learn the secrets of breadmaking, one of which is the Sicilian sea salt he puts in his breads and sells in the shop. The other is the applewood- fired brick oven Anthony uses. The shop has been open 2 1/2 years and has garnered raves from Shore food critics.

 **BEST SHOPPING**

FAIRHAVEN

Nature's Emporium. 769 River Road. (732)530-3233. Women's clothing in Indian prints and gauze, cards, crafts, and home accessories. Everything appears to be organic. Teenagers love the silver jewelry.

Sugar Plum Cottage. 803 River Road. (732)741-3364. Where baby preppies go for their smocked dresses and blazers and short pants. Very beautiful children's clothing and gift items.

EATS and TASTY TAKEOUT

Raven and the Peach. 740 River Road. (732)741-4344. A recent change of management and a new chef from France have made this one of the best restaurants in New Jersey for lunch and dinner. The food has a Gallic accent and the decor is sophisticated – even in the way the plates come out of the kitchen. Under the same roof is the **Raven Tea Room,** where lighter fare is served.

 **BEST SHOPPING**

LITTLE SILVER

Woman's Exchange of Monmouth County. 32 Church Street. (732)741-1164. Where do they get it all? Handmade baby gifts knitted by local women, hand-smocked dresses, crafts, and even apple pies and frozen hors d'oeuvres that you can take home and pop in the oven when company comes.

Byford and Mills. 50 Church Street. (732)842-5778. Owner-designer Pat Roziak has exquisite taste, which is evident in the household accessories and sensational gifts.

Mill House Antiques. 32 Willow Drive. (732)741-7411. The finest antique furniture from England, France, and America plus place settings, orientals, and outdoor statuary. More dining tables than you can imagine.

Sickles Market. Harrison Avenue (off Rumson Road). (732)741-9563. A farm market where the produce often has the dew on it from the fields and the prices aren't as high as an elephant's eye. Unusual breads and cheeses, luscious fruits, and seasonal foods. Look for annuals, perennials, and fresh flowers at all times – a giant bunch is $5.

EATS and TASTY TAKEOUT

Edie's Luncheonette. 164 Rumson Road. (732)842-9647. Hasn't changed since the '30s. Breakfast and lunch only. Try the french fries, the milkshakes, and the grilled cheese and tomato. Everyone congregates here, from the richest Rumson matrons to the contractors building their additions.

Turning Point Coffee and Tea Salon. 496 Prospect Avenue. (732)224-8718. A leisurely lunch and great dinners at this popular restaurant with new-style American cuisine.

 ## BEST SHOPPING

RUMSON

Mary Jane Roosevelt Antiques. 109 East River Road. (732)842-3159. A general line that leans toward the formal. A large selection.

Northshore of Rumson. 117 East River Road. (732)842-5533. Clothing for the active American lifestyle. Natty duds for men, sporty clothes for women. Windbreakers and pants for sailing.

Rumson China and Glass Shop. 125 East River Road. (732)842-2322. Brides love it here. In fact, everyone loves it here – a shop of fine crystal, china, silver, tablecloths, and gifts. If you are a Herend collector, you'll definitely see what you want at this glittering shop. Waterford, Baccarat, Lalique, and Orrefors in glass plus Ginori and Ceralene chinas, and Buccellati silver.

 ## EATS and TASTY TAKEOUT

Fromagerie. 26 Ridge Road. (732)842-8088. The best in French cuisine and the wines to go with at this elegant restaurant run by the Peters brothers, Hubert and Markus. Good service and old-world grace.

WORTH a DETOUR
HOLMDEL

Directions: From Red Bank, head north on Route 35.

Dearborn Farms, Inc. 2170 Route 35. **(732)264-0256.** Shoppers come from all over New Jersey to buy the fresh fruit and vegetables at Dearborn. It's especially hospitable in mid to late June when the Jersey strawberry harvest is ready and you can buy quarts reasonably for jam-making.

SHREWSBURY

Directions: Take the Garden State Parkway to exit 109 Red Bank. Follow Route 520 South to Route 35. Turn right on Route 35.

The Grove at Shrewsbury. Route 35, Shrewsbury. (732)530-1200. A well-planned mall that contains **Ann Taylor, The Gap, Banana Republic,** the excellent cottons of **Chico's,** the best in housewares and cooking utensils from **Platypus,** and hand-blocked cotton bedspreads, table mats, and napkins from **April Cornell,** among other stores.

SPRING LAKE

The picturesque seaside town of Spring Lake is unique in that year-round residents and vacationers peacefully coexist without the tension that seems to hover over so many New Jersey shore towns. Shoppers who come for the day will find more than 60 fine shops, most of them along a three-block stretch of Third Avenue from the lake (Spring Lake from whence the town gets its name) inland. Also in abundance are charming restaurants, in town or hidden away in beautifully restored small Victorian hotels, and a non-commercial boardwalk that meanders along more than a mile of spectacular beach.

Turn-of-the-century architecture is everywhere, and the lake, which is fed by underground springs and is quite clear, is bordered by path-strewn parkland.

Directions: *From North Jersey*, take the Garden State Parkway to Exit 98 and follow Route 34 south to the first traffic circle. Go three-quarters of the way around the circle to Route 524. Stay straight on Route 524, crossing over Route 35 and Route 71. When you hit Spring Lake, Route 524 becomes Ludlow Avenue. The cross streets are numbered. Take a right on Third Avenue and go four or five blocks to the central shopping district. To get to the ocean, take Ludlow to the end. *From South Jersey,* take Route I-195 East to Route 34 and follow directions from the first traffic circle.

Strategies: Spring Lake is ideal on a summer's day when you can shop and take a boardwalk stroll. Parking is all along Third Avenue and the side streets. However, the lake looks spectacular in the fall, and Christmas brings all sorts of Victorian pleasures, including a spirited weekend shopping extravaganza in early December when the town is filled with music, horse-drawn carriage rides, food vendors, and Victorian decorations. There are house tours, inn tours, and special teas.

 **BEST SHOPPING**

Kate & Company. 1100 Third Avenue. **(732)449-1633**. On the corner by the lake, this glistening home furnishings shop has furniture, accessories, and gifts from all over the world. From England, battery-driven clocks whose faces reflect golf, tennis, sailing, and other sports themes. Glass from Mexico, good-looking Irish pine, upholstered pieces, candles, lamps and lighting.

The Moon & Sixpence. 1104 Third Avenue. **(732)449-0556**. A dreamy little shop, this store specializes in painted furniture, art, jewelry, and items for the home. Some unique pieces, especially the furniture.

Third Avenue Chocolate Shoppe. 1118 Third Avenue. **(732)449-7535**. Candymaker Matt Magyar offers truly extraordinary chocolates year round, all but a few handmade on the premises. He shines brightest, though, at Christmas, Valentine's Day, and Easter when out come the chocolate-covered pretzels and the mouth-watering coated pretzel sticks known as chicken legs. There are also turtles, caramels, fudge, nonpareils, butter crunch, and rich dark and milk chocolate forms. Don't go away without trying the giant malted milk balls that Matt imports from a candymaker in Brooklyn. They come in white and dark chocolate, coffee, raspberry, and other flavors. Open seven days. Handsome gift wrapping.

Courts and Greens. 1209 Third Avenue. **(732)449-1844**. When you see a unusually well dressed woman teeing off and wonder where she shops, it's probably at Courts and Greens. The boutique carries golf skirts and shorts, matching sweaters, tennis dresses, and separates that range from adorable to elegant. Accessories are great-looking, too. Putting together a coordinated outfit can be on the high side, but how can you put a price tag on style?

Teddy Bears By The Seashore. 1306 Third Avenue (adult resortwear), 317 Morris Avenue (infantwear, girls, and boys). (732)449-7446. Casual clothes, sweatshirts, tees, khaki slacks, and bears all around. These are apparel outlets where clothing for the family is discounted. They open late and close early (11 a.m. to 4 p.m.), but are open 7 days.

Sweet Pea. 1311 Third Avenue. (732)449-6999. Whether your decor is classic or modern, the home accessories at Sweet Pea fit in with every decorating style. This light-filled shop carries Italian and French dinnerware, exquisite lamps, linens, cocktail table books, birdhouses, and more. Peek under and around everything. There are treasures to be unearthed.

Spring Lace. 221 Morris Avenue. (732)449-0021. Lace curtains in dozens of patterns, from dainty window liners to billowy drapery. Also fine table linens, items for tea, and gifts with an antique look. A small shop but packed with goodies.

 EATS and TASTY TAKEOUT

The Sandpiper. 7 Atlantic Avenue. (732)449-4700. Steps from the boardwalk, the romantic Sandpiper Inn has an excellent casual restaurant open for lunch and dinner. The Sunday brunch, served from 11 a.m. to 2:30 p.m., is sumptuous. Make reservations. If you want to drink, bring your own.

Who's On Third Deli-Grill. 1300 Third Avenue. (732)449-4233. Booths and tables sprawl out over several rooms, the place to go for well-prepared sandwiches, fresh turkey, and good burgers.

 **WORTH a DETOUR**

OCEAN GROVE

Located across Lake Wesley just south of Asbury Park, Victorian Ocean Grove is a camp meeting ground grown up. The brightly colored houses with their gingerbread architecture and tent cottages are vestiges of the prayer resort founded by Methodists in 1869. They surround the Great Auditorium, which was built in 1894 as a "preacher's stand" and holds 6,500 people. The shopping district along Main Avenue and the streets leading to the Great Auditorium are lined with charming stores, restaurants, bakeries, and antique shops. Ocean Grove is one square mile, so park along Main and walk.

Directions: *From Spring Lake,* follow Route 71 North to the outskirts of Asbury Park. Go past the light at the intersection of Route 33 and look for the entrance to Ocean Grove on the right.

From the Garden State Parkway, take Exit 100 Asbury Park. Get on Route 33 South and follow it about 5 miles until it ends at Route 71 (Main Street). Turn left on Route 71 and go down a few blocks. The entrance to Ocean Grove is on the right.

 EATS and TASTY TAKEOUT

The Raspberry Cafe. 60 Main Avenue. **(732)988-0833.** Open May to September. Excellent for lunch, tea, or just juice.

DEAL

Directions: *From Ocean Grove,* head north on Route 71 across Deal Lake into Deal. Detour to the ocean to see some of the most magnificent homes in New Jersey. When you reach Roosevelt Avenue, turn left, then left again on Route 71

(Norwood Avenue) for the shopping district.

Pitti Bimi. 264 Norwood Avenue. (732)531-3676. A couturier shop for children, newborn to age 14. Imported from France, Italy, and England, the mini-fashions at Pitti Bimi are both adorable and elegant, but pricey. This is where to shop for flower girl dresses. The layette selection, with its fine cottons and bedding, is for the privileged infant.

WEST END-LONG BRANCH

Directions: *From Deal,* head north on Ocean Avenue into Long Branch.

From the Garden State Parkway, get off at Exit 105 Eatontown and head south on Route 36 to Ocean Avenue.

Block China Outlet Store. 57-B Brighton Avenue. (732)222-1144. Just steps off Ocean Avenue, this discount outlet "find" invites the customer to come "be a bull in a china shop." And there's a lot to be bullish about here. Block brand china is handsome and well made. Dinner sets, individual pieces, and large ceramic bowls can be found in abundance. The barware and crystal are gorgeous, especially the large glass pieces. Savings are up to 70 percent off retail. A super place to purchase engagement or wedding gifts. Open seven days.

 EATS and TASTY TAKEOUT

Windmill Restaurant. 586 Ocean Avenue. (732)229-9863. This small restaurant, located around the corner from the Block China Outlet, is known for its grilled hot dogs. The frankfurters are long enough to protrude from their squeezably soft rolls and are delicious — naked or with the works.

WESTFIELD

Westfield seems to be a town in transition. There is Westfield the up-scale village, with Gaps and Express stores, fancy shoe boutiques, a Starbucks, and a handful of trendy eateries. Then there is the other Westfield – old-fashioned family-owned shops and funky antique stores with a department store like Lord & Taylor thrown in for good measure. In any event, Westfield is the perfect place to do holiday shopping because it has as much variety as a major mall without the controlled atmosphere of a mall.

Directions: *From the Garden State Parkway,* take Exit 135 at Clark onto Central Avenue and follow it into the center of Westfield.

From Route 22, take Mountain Avenue at the entrance to Echo Lake County Park. It will intersect with Broad Street, the main thoroughfare of Westfield. Turn right and find parking.

Strategies: Except perhaps at holiday time, one can usually park on the street in Westfield. Parking on Broad, Elm, Quimby, and Prospect streets is metered and shoppers dart in and out. But if you can't find a spot on the street, head for the lots behind the Broad Street stores. These are almost always half full. Start your shopping in town, then get in the car and drive to Lord & Taylor or the antique shops along Central Avenue.

 **BEST SHOPPING**

Brummer's Homemade Chocolates. 125 East Broad Street. (908)232-1904. All the chocolates are made on the premises the old-fashioned way. Other interesting candies include the multi-colored all-day suckers and small spearmint leaves.

Recipes Inc. and Temptations. 131 East Broad Street. (908)654-4999. All the fancy cooking equipment and utensils a gourmet cook could need cheek by jowl with a shop that sells exciting dinnerware and serving pieces.

Garden Botanika. 200 East Broad Street (at the corner of Elm Street). (908)789-8353. Peer in the window and get mesmerized by the jars and vials of natural plant-based ingredients that make up the cosmetic and home products sold at this wonderful shop.

Gap and Gap Kids. 207 and 234 East Broad Street. (908)654-8260 and (908)233-2723. Both larger stores in the Gap chain, well-merchandised and well run.

Betty Gallagher Antiques, Inc. 266 East Broad Street. (908)654-4222. Two floors of exquisite formal and country furniture, lamps, china, and glassware, all elegant. Definitely look at the jewelry.

MaryLou's Memorabilia and Collectibles. 17 Elm Street. (908)654-7277. If you remember the Lone Ranger or Howdy Doody, collect Mickey Mouse, or love lunchboxes from the '60s, don't miss MaryLou's for variety. It makes you smile just to go in.

Storytime on Elm. 35 Elm Street. (908)232-1343. A terrific store for kids where you'll find unusual books, toys, and music. Great for birthday gifts.

House of Legacies. 53 Elm Street. (908)518-1700. This place is by appointment only, but if you are going to Westfield, it is worth a visit to see the vintage Cartier, Patek Philippe, and Rolex watches; the Tiffany jewelry; and the diamond engagement rings.

Scott's Shoes of Westfield. 101 Quimby Street (near Central Avenue). (908)233-5678. A very up-scale shoe shop for men and women, with lots of Italian imports and the finest American-made shoes.

Linda Elmore Antiques. 395 Cumberland (at the corner of South Avenue). (908)233-5443. Furniture of all periods, but early 20th century is the specialty here. Nice decorative accessories.

The Sock Company. 719 Central Avenue. (908)232-4333. A branch of a small discount chain with stores in Montvale, Bergenfield, Toms River, Emerson, and Wyckoff, the Sock Company has a fantastic selection of socks, underwear, hosiery, Jansport backpacks, hats, lingerie, and Lee jeans. Among the brands they carry are No Fear, Vanity Fair, Warner's, Danskin, Berkshire, Hot Sox, Wigwam, and Champion.

Lord & Taylor. 609 North Avenue. (908)233-6600. A freestanding Lord & Taylor with well-stocked men's, ladies', and children's clothing departments as well as cosmetic counters, gifts, and even a restaurant. The sales staff is extremely friendly.

 # EATS and TASTY TAKEOUT

Lia's. 27 Elm Street. (908)654-0045. One of the smallest yet best food take-out shops in all New Jersey. The accent is Italian, but the menu selection will fit every palate. Eat in or take out. Roasted vegetables, pasta salads, grilled Portobello mushrooms, chicken done dozens of ways, and delectable and unusual breads from New York's best bakeries. Don't miss the gelato.

Mojave Grille. 235 North Avenue (near the intersection of Elm Street). (908)232-7772. This restaurant has smashing decor. Southwestern specialties are served. Excellent for lunch Monday through Friday, but the restaurant does not serve lunch on weekends.

Vivian's Kitchen. 10 Prospect Street. (908)654-6995. It's lunch, a bakery with delicious cookies and muffins, and an antique shop all in one. Dynamite sandwiches.

Northside Trattoria. 16 Prospect Street. (908)232-7320. A fun place for lunch. Pastas, gourmet pizzas with an excellent new-style crust, and inventive salads.

 **WORTH a DETOUR**

MOUNTAINSIDE

Directions: From Broad Street in Westfield, take Mountain Avenue toward Route 22. Mountainside begins after Mountain Avenue's intersection with North Chestnut Street.

Christoffers Flowers. 860 Mountain Avenue. (908)233-0500. This is one of the best florists in New Jersey, turning out inventive and creative arrangements on the spur of the moment. The space next door carries beautiful containers, tablecloths and placemats, and neat gifts.

SCOTCH PLAINS

Directions: From Westfield, travel west on Broad Street, but do not go under the train tracks. Stay straight on Broad, which becomes North Avenue before Lord & Taylor. Go to the T-intersection at Martine Avenue and turn right. Go straight on Martine. Eventually it becomes Park Avenue, the main street of Scotch Plains.

Stage House Antiques Center. 364 Park Avenue. (908)322-2311. Many dealers show their wares here and you will find a lot of formal china plus art glass and the English chintz transferware that has become so popular. Prices are moderate. Not open Mondays.

Richard Roberts Ltd. 375 Park Avenue. (908)322-5535. This unusual store combines furniture, linens, and home decor.

SHORTER SHOPPING TRIPS in CENTRAL NEW JERSEY

CLINTON

A slice of rural America located in Hunterdon County, Clinton has an old red mill, a meandering river, and a charming Main Street where strolling is encouraged.

Directions: Take Route 78 West to the Route 31 North exit. After leaving the exit ramp, go 100 yards and turn right where it says Clinton. Bear right over the highway through a traffic light and straight into town on Route 173.

After the second traffic light (Leigh Street), turn right at the Clinton House restaurant. Make a right onto the old bridge over the Raritan River. You will be on Main Street. There is on-street parking and a lot behind the stores along the left side of the street.

 **BEST SHOPPING**

Twelve Main Street. 12 Main Street. (908)735-2274. A funky shop with natural women's clothing, candles, jewelry, and home furnishings.

Memories. 21 Main Street. (908)730-9096. A group antique shop with some nice oak furniture, oils and prints, china, and Depression glass.

Alternatives. 8-A Leigh Street. (908)735-6661. This floral shop combined with antiques, jewelry, and contemporary designs is one of Hunterdon County's most interesting. Ideas spring from the fertile brain of proprietor Tony Martino.

Stone Mill Shop. 7 Lower Center Street. (908)730-8780. Located inside the Hunterdon Art Center, this shop stocks the finest contemporary ceramics, blown glass, wall hangings, and other crafts. Many pieces are from artists who have exhibited at the art center.

COLUMBUS

This is the heart of New Jersey's "salad bowl," with farm after farm producing luscious vegetables in season.

Directions: Get off the New Jersey Turnpike at Exit 7. Pay the toll and head south on Route 206. Go 5 miles to reach Columbus.

 **BEST SHOPPING**

Columbus Farmers Market and Flea Market. 2919 Route 206. (609)267-0400. This sprawling market complex may seem to be in an obscure location, but it is just off Exit 7 of the New Jersey Turnpike. The goods, produce, and greenery market is open Thursday through Sunday starting at dawn, and the flea market is open Thursday, Saturday, and Sunday starting at dawn. So you may want to hit it on a weekend when both are going strong. Vendors start going home by 1 p.m., so get an early start! The flea market is to the left of the permanent buildings. The produce section is in open stalls at the other end of the market. Here you will see bulk fruits and vegetables – you cannot buy just one or two pieces. The jumbo eggs are right off the farm, the mozzarella is fresh, and the Italian bread is squeezable. In summer, the produce is all Jersey grown.

The permanent buildings house stalls selling everything from ladies' clothing and antiques to old records and toys. Don't miss the space dedicated to the butchered meats, baking, and crafts of Amish farmers. The barbecued chickens are wonderful and the pretzel stand serves a hotdog with cheese wrapped in pretzel dough that could be one of the best eats in America! Wash it down with fresh lemonade.

Garden vendors offer reasonably priced shrubs, annuals, and perennials.

WASHINGTON

This borough, once filled with prosperous mills, fell on hard times in the 1960s. However, the recent conversion of area farms to housing developments seems to have sparked a rejuvenation.

Directions: Take I-78 West to Clinton, exiting onto Route 31 North. Take Route 31 North to Washington, about 11 miles. At the traffic light at

the intersection of Route 31 and Route 57, turn
left. Go west on Route 57. After the Bagelsmith,
go right at the traffic light at Brasscastle Road.

 **BEST SHOPPING**

Castle Creek Mill End Shop. 47C Brasscastle
Road. (908)689-7848. A real find for its collection
of Waverly upholstery and drapery fabrics well
below retail. Designer fabric from other mills
carried as well.

SOUTHERN
NEW JERSEY

CAPE MAY

There's something about a house painted tastefully in red, cream, lilac, apricot, and forest green that makes you smile. Well, one does a lot of that in Cape May where dozens of once-crumbling Victorian homes have been spruced up and turned into attractive bed-and-breakfasts for the bike and brunch trade. Shopkeepers have also set up amid the gingerbread, selling everything from antiques and crafts to high-fashion clothing and flowers. It doesn't take a cloudy day to bring out the buyers. Everybody seems to sunbathe in the morning and shop and dine in the early afternoon!

Don't ignore some of the other Cape May attractions, such as the tours of the historic Cape May Lighthouse in Cape May Point State Park (climb the 199 stairs to the top for a panoramic view) or a walk through the purportedly ghost-infested Emlen Physick Estate at 1049 Washington Street.

Directions: *From North Jersey,* take the Garden State Parkway to its southern terminus. Get on Route 109 South and enter Cape May along Lafayette Avenue. Go half a mile, bear left onto Bank Street, then left again to Jackson Street. Go several blocks to the Washington Street pedestrian mall.

From South Jersey, take Route 42 South to Route 55 South through Vineland. Follow signs to Route 47-347 South. After passing through the community known as Cape May Courthouse, look for Seashore Road on your right. Bear right onto Seashore Road and cross the Cape May Canal. At this point, Seashore Road becomes Broadway. At Broadway and West Perry, make a left and go down several blocks to the Washington Street pedestrian mall.

Strategies: Cape May is not the easiest town for parking. There are metered lots behind the Washington Street stores, so look for these first. Metered parking is also available on Ocean Street from the beach up. If all else fails, there is paid parking in the lot of the Acme Market on Ocean Street at Washington. You will be reimbursed if you buy something at the town shops.

Walk the three blocks of the Washington Street pedestrian mall, then hit the newly refurbished Congress Hall and its terrific shops. This grand hotel was the summer White House to President Benjamin Harrison. When you have finished exploring the pedestrian mall, saunter down Perry to The Promenade along Beach Drive and head east to Queen Street, stopping to see the fabulously painted Victorian homes. Detour up Ocean Street for some interesting shops and houses. When you've walked enough, get in the car and head west out of town toward the Lighthouse, pausing at the antique shops on Broadway.

A side trip takes you to Historic Cold Spring Village, an outdoor living history museum on Route 9, (609)898-2300. Garden enthusiasts will want to tour the 25 different gardens on a one-mile circuit within Leaming's Run Gardens in Swainton, (609)465-5871.

 **BEST SHOPPING**

C.B. South. 251 Beach Drive (at the Shops of Congress Hall). **(609)884-7570.** An inviting women's apparel store where the fashions are current and super comfortable. The shop carries brands such as PA Company, Kiko, and Michael Stors.

Love The Cook. Perry Street and Congress Place (at the Shops of Congress Hall). **(609)884-**

9292. Kitchen gadgets, gourmet ingredients, cookbooks. In all over 10,000 items for the cook in the family.

Sea Dragon Herbery. Perry Street and Congress Place (at the Shops of Congress Hall). **(609)884-4858.** The smell of this unique flower shop is intoxicating! Dozens of drying flowers hang from the ceiling and arrangements in stunning containers are all around. Unusual fresh flowers from their fields in West Cape May in season. Custom orders a specialty.

The Market at Bubbling Well Road. 411 Washington Mall. **(609)884-1935.** A crafts gallery with handwrought silver jewelry, pottery, wind chimes, and sculpture. Calming music plays while you shop. Has a very Zen feeling.

Weekend Sports. Carpenter's Lane and Perry Street (in Carpenter's Square Mall). **(609)399-2137.** If you are looking for a better tee shirt or long-sleeved top with the Cape May moniker, stop in at this inviting shop. Also, custom monogramming on towels, canvas boat bags, etc., while you wait.

Cheeks at the Beach. 101 Ocean Avenue (at Columbia Street). **(609)884-8484.** Trendy clothes for the younger woman, bathing suits and strappy tees in season, and sweaters and slacks for when the days get colder. Some very wonderful gift items.

Hazard-Sealander. 479 West Perry Street. **(609)884-0040.** One of the few antique shops where smalls, china, and glass are not featured. Look for furniture, outdoor urns, lamps, and other larger items. The owners also have the stunning ***Acquisitions*** shop in the ***Congress Hall Ballroom,*** **(609)884-0006.** It carries dining room tables, sofas, and outdoor statuary.

Rocking Horse Antiques Center. 405 Perry Street. **(609)898-0737.** A group shop with more than 40 dealers. Open 7 days. Some nice Victorian silver, English bone china, linens, old sand pails, and smaller pieces of furniture.

Finestkind. 139 Broadway. (609)898-1622. An antique shop carrying vintage clothing, '30s china, regional folk art, and nostalgia. At the back, Brenda West Wolfe stitches up gorgeous pillows and bridal accessories such as ringbearer pillows and bridal money bags in her new shop, **Accurate Stitches & Design.**

Bogwater Jim. 201 Broadway. (609)884-5558. The maritime antiques and artifacts are very special. The owner stocks sailing vessel primitives that would look terrific in a seashore house!

Cape May Linen Outlet. 110 Park Boulevard (next to Cape May Lumber). (609)884-3630. A little outside Cape May center, but worth it. Excellent prices on sheets such as Fieldcrest's Charisma and Court de Versailles. Handsome comforters and Fieldcrest and Cannon towels in rich colors. Buy your beach towels here! Table linens as well.

Cape Island Antiques. 609 Jefferson Street. (609)884-6028. More than 2,500 square feet of American Victoriana and other fine antiques. Lots of marble-topped dressing tables and boudoir chairs.

 EATS and TASTY TAKEOUT

Mad Batter. 19 Jackson Street. (609)884-5970. Just up the street from the beach, the Mad Batter attracts quite a crowd to its front porch and rear garden with its cuisine based on fresh foods and incomparable desserts. The top brunch spot in Cape May.

Two Mile Crab House. Two Mile Landing (on Ocean Drive between Cape May and Wildwood). (609)522-1341. The dining is casual and water views from the outdoor deck are lovely. Order anything with crab, particularly the spicy Maryland crabs and the crabcake sandwiches.

VanScoy's Bistro. Carpenter's Lane and Perry Street (behind the Pink House in Carpenter's

Square Mall). **(609)898-9898.** Light fare for lunch. Exceptional salads, good cappuccino. Dine outside or in.

WORTH a DETOUR
GREEN CREEK

Directions: This area is 11 miles from Cape May. From town, take Broadway out toward Cape May Point. As you head inland, cross over Cape May Canal. The road name changes to Seashore Road. At the junction of Seashore Road and Route 47, turn left and go north 8 miles to Green Creek.

Marlboro Farm Market. **Route 47 (in Middle Township). (609)886-2524.** Shop at this fine farm market for the most incredible annuals in spring and summer. You'll appreciate the low prices, too. Luscious summer produce straight from the farm. Mums and pumpkins in fall.

MAURICETOWN

Don't miss the charming little town of Mauricetown on the Maurice River, a tributary to the Delaware. This is a virtually undiscovered area of New Jersey, and antiquers will find it merits visiting. There are six antique shops in town. Three antique shows a year are held at the firehouse. The best one takes place in early December. Mauricetown is also where you can see the sport of railbirding, an unusual practice in which dogs paddle out to the river rice paddies to retrieve railbirds bagged by hunters.

Directions: Mauricetown is off Route 47, about 16 miles north of Green Creek. When you see the Mauricetown signs, turn left onto Mauricetown Road and go about 1 1/2 miles to Highland Street. To get to Front Street, turn left on Highland and right on Front. To reach the other shops, turn right on Highland Street.

Boxwood & Ivy. **9087 Highland Street.**

(609)785-1246. A shop with high-end goods, exquisite Majolica, silver, furniture, and decorative accessories. An annex has more primitive things.

Cook House Antiques. 9533 Highland Street. **(609)785-1137.** Has a nice variety of china and smalls.

Tulip Tree Antiques. End of Front Street at South Street. No phone. Set amidst charming gardens, a general line of antiques.

Campbell's Flea Market. Route 47 at the Texaco Station (past the turnoff to Heislerville). **No phone.** This small flea market operates on Saturday and Sunday in good weather. The offerings are a mixed bag of old and new, antiques and junk.

CHERRY HILL, MARLTON, and VOORHEES

Although it is all highway driving and darting in and out of malls, the shopping in this region is excellent. Many of Philadelphia's best shops have outposts here and the Voorhees area is rapidly becoming one of Camden County's poshest suburbs, with new malls and stores opening at a dizzying pace. But go a few miles off the highways and you'll find bucolic countryside.

Directions: *From Trenton,* take Route 295 South to Route 70.

From the New Jersey Turnpike, get off at Exit 4, then follow Route 73 South to its intersection with Route 70.

Strategies: Most of the best shopping in this region is sited along the eastbound and westbound lanes of Routes 70 and 73 in Cherry Hill, Marlton, and Voorhees. Perhaps the best way to tackle this 10-mile stretch is to start around the Garden State Race Track on Route 70 and head east to Marlton and Voorhees, picking up Route 73 at Olga's Diner. Turn around at Voorhees and do the stores on the west side of Route 70. An interesting place to visit is the Barclay Farmstead Museum, Barclay Road, Cherry Hill, (609)795-6225. It offers tours of a 19th-century house and outbuildings. Scarborough Covered Bridge is nearby.

 **BEST SHOPPING**

CHERRY HILL

Garden State Park Flea Market. Route 70 Westbound and Cornell Avenue. (609)665-8558. On the grounds of Garden State Park, this flea market is open Wednesday and Sunday March through December. Clothing, tools, jewelry, plants, handbags, and toys.

JDR Shoe Warehouse. 16 North Springdale Road (behind the Garden State Discovery Museum). (609)751-6668. Moderate to expensive shoes at substantial discounts. Where to come when you need a navy blue flat to wear with pants or a pair or loafers and don't want to spend an arm and a leg for them. The warehouse carries brands such as Via Spiga, Aigner, Nine West, Franco Sarto, and Enzo. Open only Friday and Saturday from 10 a.m. to 6 p.m. and Sunday from 11 a.m. to 5 p.m.

I. Goldberg. 1629 Route 70 Westbound and Kings Highway. (609)795-2244. What can't you find here? A supermarket of everything from surplus clothing, work gear, and hiking footwear to camping and leisure-time equipment.

Jack Kellmer Co. Route 70 Eastbound and Kings Highway. (609)795-3500. The area's widest selection of jewelry and watches like Tag Heuer and Rolex. Wonderful giftware section that should be visited if you need wedding gifts.

Robinson Discount Luggage. 1422 Route 70 Westbound (in Pine Tree Plaza). (609)751-0700. Discounts of as much as 60 percent on luggage, among the brands sleek Tumi, perky Lark, and the cost-conscious Boyt, Delsey, and Travel Pro. Robinson carries all the latest pull-bags with retractable handles. Also, the biggest duffles you've ever seen (perfect for camp), backpacks, and carriers for computers, or just about anything else you might want to take along.

Sym's. 1865 Route 70 Eastbound. (609)424-0884. See Secaucus entry for a description.

 EATS and TASTY TAKEOUT

Big John's Steaks, Pizza & Deli. 1800 Route 70 East, Cherry Hill. (609)424-1186. A casual place with the best cheesesteaks this side of Philly. Only now, with a nod to healthy eating, you can have your cheesesteak made with chicken.

Norma's Middle Eastern Restaurant. 145 Route 70 (in Barclay Farms Shopping Center), Cherry Hill. (609)795-1373. On the menu are authentic hummus, baba ghanoush, falafel, and even schwarma, a Middle East savory made with lamb scraps. Desserts are sweet and worth it.

 **BEST SHOPPING**

MARLTON

Sweetly Yours. 157 Route 73 South (in Marlton Crossing Shopping Center). (609)983-4344. A confectionery shop that has a wide variety of chocolates, nuts, and sinful chocolate-covered pretzels. Give as gifts or take home all for yourself. Cookies, coffee, everything for baskets.

Smith Bros. 237 Route 73 South (in Marlton Crossing Shopping Center). (609)985-6433. Well-designed clothing for teenagers and young women, at eminently reasonable prices. Trendy dresses, mostly casual wear.

Kamikaze Kids. 501 Route 73 South (in Town Place at Marlton). (609)983-1100. Upscale children's shop with European imports and nearly the entire Flapdoodles line. Some toys and gifts for kids, too.

Zagara's and Zagara's Home. 501 Route 73 South (in Town Place at Marlton). (609)983-5700. One of the most fabulous gourmet shops outside Manhattan. Come in and be wowed by the bakery, breaderie, fish counter, butcher, the cheeses, prepared foods, sauces and pastas, the produce, and the flowers. In-store coffee bar. Adjacent, **Zagara's Home** is loaded with wonderful china, gifts, candles, and even antiques and furniture.

Asta De Blue. 515 Route 73 South (in the Borders Mall). (609)985-0700. The clothes are European and high-fashion American. The shoes are au courant and the handbags and accessories are irresistible. One-stop shopping for an outfit, especially one for an important occasion.

Zany Brainy. 515 Route 73 South (in the Borders Mall). (609)596-0093. You don't have to be a brainy kid (or adult) to adore this store. The best educational toys, games, craft projects, and books.

 EATS and TASTY TAKEOUT

Champps. 25 Route 73 South (in the Marlton Crossing Shopping Center), Marlton. (609)985-9333. A restaurant with sports bar. Dine while more than a dozen televisions surround you with action. Light cuisine, including great burgers and sandwiches, pastas, fajitas. Everyone starts with the crab bread.

Joe's Peking Duck House. Route 73 South (in the Marlton Crossing Shopping Center), Marlton. (609)985-1551. A well-prepared, reasonable lunch Monday through Friday.

BEST SHOPPING

VOORHEES

China Outlet & Gourmet Garage. 993 Route 73 South (in Designers Court). (609)988-0333 or 1-800-853-3472. Another branch of this store is located at 443 Shore Road, Somers Point. 1-800-538-6208. Everyday china; wineglasses; gourmet cookware from Calphalon, Anolon, and Circulon; and oodles of gourmet foods and sauces are for sale in this spacious store. Excellent prices on appliances from Krups, Braun, Proctor-Silex, and Cuisinart. You'll find open stock of new Fiestaware at prices Macy's or Bloomingdale's cannot begin to match.

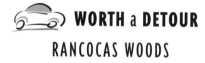

WORTH a DETOUR

RANCOCAS WOODS

Directions: Take I-295 to the exit for Rancocas Woods (Exit 43). Follow the Rancocas Woods sign onto Creek Road and go south 1 mile.

Rancocas Woods Flea Market. Creek Road. (609)235-1830. A flea market held on the second Sunday of each month from March through December, Rancocas Creek offers the wares of 160 antique dealers in a wooded setting. Hours are 8 a.m. to 3 p.m., but the dealers are out in force early and some pack up to go home by 1 or 2 p.m. Trenton pottery, in its distinctive pale colors, is in ample supply, as is old Stangl pottery, which was made in Flemington. Lots of vintage linens, costume jewelry, comic books, and other collectibles. The prices are excellent. When you are finished, browse the shops of the small village.

JACKSON

The scrub pine country of New Jersey isn't beautiful, atmospheric, or endearing. But it is accessible, thanks to a new road, I-195, that went through nearly two decades ago. Six Flags Great Adventure Theme Park and Safari, with its animals of the African veldt and its stomach-churning Batman ride, was the first to draw tourists to the area. Now, the 195,000 square-foot Six Flags Factory Outlets, a collection of 50 name-brand stores, are reeling in visitors at the juncture of Route 537 (Monmouth Road) and Anderson Road. A second section, more than 100,000 square feet in size, opened in April. The main number for the outlets is (732)833-0680.

Directions: *From New Jersey Turnpike,* take Exit 7A to I-195 East. Get off at Exit 16A for the amusement park, Six Flags Great Adventure, and 16B for Six Flags Factory Outlets.

From the Garden State Parkway, get off at Exit 98, then take I-195 West to Exit 16.

Strategies: If the kids are with you, one parent or chaperone should hang out at the amusement park while the other shops! To get from Great Adventure to the outlets, take Monmouth Road back the way you came, past the entrances to I-195, and the outlets will be on the right. They stay open until 9 p.m. Dine in the food court or at one of the several restaurants along Monmouth Road, including McDonald's. A free shuttle bus also runs between the outlets and the theme park.

 **BEST SHOPPING**

Liz Claiborne Shoes. Store #134 (Six Flags Factory Outlets). (732)928-6401. This national retailer has just a few stores like this across the country. Heels, pumps, flats, and sneakers like you would find at Nordstrom's or any other large department store. Fashionable without being trendy. Most shoes are in the $30 to $60 range, about half what they'd be regular retail. The shop also carries wonderful handbags.

Maternity Works. Store #140 (Six Flags Factory Outlets). (732)833-0662. A discount shop carrying expensive brands like Mimi Maternity and Motherhood. A huge selection at savings of 30 to 50 percent.

Donna Karan Company Store. Store #142 (Six Flags Factory Outlets). (732)928-0800. See Flemington entry for a description.

Florsheim Factory Outlet. Store #151 (Six Flags Factory Outlets). (732)833-1086. Handsome all-leather men's shoes, from elegant loafers to shoes a business executive could wear. Prices about 40 to 50 percent off regular stores.

Big Dog Sportswear. Store #154 (Six Flags Factory Outlets). (732)833-0300. All the great shorts, tees, polos, and underwear from this exciting West Coast manufacturer of surfing wear. Great for teenage boys! One of two Big Dog outlets in New Jersey (the other is in Secaucus), this store is crammed with Big Dog items like eyewear, huge plushy beach towels, and even mouse pads. Their clothing for infants and toddlers is adorable.

Pfaltzgraff. Store #192 (Six Flags Factory Outlets). (732)928-6666. See Flemington entry for a description.

Starter. Store #200 (Six Flags Factory Outlets). (732)255-5755. Children and teenagers of both sexes will adore this store and its "with-it" merchandise carrying the logos of America's top sport teams. Jackets, shorts, tee shirts, and warm-up wear.

J. Crew. Store #208 (Six Flags Factory Outlets). (732)928-8777. There are only two J. Crew stores in New Jersey (Short Hills Mall and Garden State Plaza in Paramus), but this is the first outlet in the Garden State. The usual good buys on cotton shirts, shorts, and pants for women and men. Some of J. Crew's better women's silks here. Look for cashmere sweaters in winter.

Note: Some of the other shops at Six Flags include *Calvin Klein, Gap Factory Store, XOXO, Jockey Factory Store, London Fog Factory Store, Reebok Factory Outlet, Timberland, Black & Decker, Harry & David, KB Toy Outlet,* and *Nautica.* The Nautica store features one of only two Nautica Boys outlets in the country.

LONG BEACH ISLAND
and MAINLAND towns of
BARNEGAT,
MANAHAWKIN, and
TUCKERTON

Many New Jerseyans spent their childhood summers on the white sands of Long Beach Island, an 18-mile-long barrier island crammed nearly end to end with shops, eateries, and miniature golf courses. Barnegat and Manahawkin along Route 9 don't have much in the way of serious shopping, but select shops are very appealing. Then it's south on Route 9 to Tuckerton and beyond where antiques, farm markets, and clam bars just wait to be discovered.

Directions: To LBI, get off at Exit 63 of the Garden State Parkway. Take Route 72 south through Manahawkin, over Barnegat Bay Bridge to the traffic circle. Turn right for Beach Haven and left for Surf City, Harvey Cedars, and Barnegat Light.

On the mainland, the village of Barnegat is three or four miles above Manahawkin.

Tuckerton is down Route 9 about 10 miles, traveling toward Atlantic City.

Strategies: Wait for a rainy day. Or don't. Drive from Holgate to Barnegat Light. Picnic, fish, and visit Old Barney at Barnegat Lighthouse State Park, located at the northernmost tip of LBI in Barnegat Light, (609)494-2016. Another lousy day? It can happen. Head off-island for some shopping adventures. There's the charming settlement of Barnegat, with its little old-fashioned Main Street; the Barnegat Friends Meeting House on East Bay Avenue; the Historical Museum (open Saturdays and Sundays from 1 to 4 p.m.); and the open waters of Barnegat Bay at the end of East Bay Avenue where the marinas and beaches are. In summer, farmstands packed with homegrown Jersey produce line Route 9.

BEST SHOPPING

LONG BEACH ISLAND

Bay Village & Schooner's Wharf. 9th and Bay Avenue, Beach Haven. **(609)492-2800** or **(609)492-4400.** More than 50 darling shops here in an old-time fishing village format. Everything is connected by boardwalks and brick patios. Free parking on site. Meet at the ship, made in the image of the historic schooner Lucy Evelyn, which anchored at this spot in 1948 and served as a mercantile establishment until it burned 20 years ago. Today, there are tee shirt shops, silver jewelry shops, a **Crabtree & Evelyn** shop, craft galleries, bakeries, fudge shops, and restaurants. Sidewalk carts sell tye-died items, socks, and hair ornaments. There's even a place where you can surf the Internet by the hour!

Sur La Plage. 10th Street and Bay Avenue, Beach Haven. (609)492-4440. Another location at 19th Street and Long Beach Boulvard, Surf City. (609)494-7500. Hip clothing and shoes that appeal to teens and the college set. For women, Esprit and Guess are big. For men, there are the surfer lines like Stussy and Billabong.

The Hand Store. 14th Street and Bay Avenue, Beach Haven. (609)492-2385. Another location at 25th Street and Long Beach Boulevard, Ship Bottom. (609)494-5212. To enter a Hand's is to enter a realm where everything a shore homeowner might need is within arm's reach. This is the first stop for visitors because of the selection of beach chairs, chaises, umbrellas, etc. There are lamps, kitchen cookware, mini-blinds, boat hardware, toys, sheets and towels, grills, and surprisingly nice swimsuits and clothing for all ages. An old-fashioned store with lots of sales help on hand to answer questions.

Bikini Headquarters. 126 North Bay Avenue, Beach Haven. (609)492-8322. Fantastic selection of handmade bikini bathing suits. The great thing is you can buy them as separates, so if you are larger on top than you are on the bottom, or vice versa, just pick out the one that fits. Four different bra styles and three different brief styles. Fabric is high-quality stretch in beautiful prints and solids. The women who work here are really helpful. If you see something and it's not available in your size, they will have it made up in a few days.

Summerhouse. 412 North Bay Avenue, Beach Haven. (609)492-6438. A blend of new and old. Antiques, tablewear, furniture, candles, gifts, all perfect for summer living. Small shop with a large selection of merchandise. Nice sales help.

La Paloma. 4 West Maryland Avenue at Long Beach Boulevard, Beach Haven Terrace. **(609)492-2373.** This is a block of shopping, all owned by the same person, with a hair salon and high-fashion women's clothing. The shop carries lovely suits and dresses plus a line of lingerie called La Perla that is only carried by a few shops in the East. The bras, underwear, and nightgowns are simply exquisite. The owner has customers from as far away as Hawaii!

The Leather Warehouse. Kentucky Avenue and Long Beach Boulevard, Haven Beach. **(609)492-0669.** Where other Leather Warehouses have closed across New Jersey, this discount outpost remains open. The shop carries leathers and suedes of high quality at prices that are truly affordable. The shearling coats are particularly nice. So are the handbags. Open: June, July, and August. Another location in Shrewsbery open all year, 1-800-953-2843.

Sink'r Swim Shop. South Carolina Avenue and Long Beach Boulevard, Haven Beach. **(609)492-4554.** LBI's premier shop for men's and ladies' clothing. Some women we know make it a habit of stopping here on Memorial Day every year to purchase a bathing suit for the summer. Sink'r Swim has more than any store on the island. Hundreds of Gottexes, Jantzens, and Adrienne Vittadinis plus every major manufacturer. Also beautiful coverups, gauzy casual clothing, slacks, golf wear, and accessories.

Wizard of Odds. 7601 Long Beach Boulevard, Beach Haven Crest. **(609)492-9384.** An eclectic collection of antiques, from early Shore-iana to silver, dolls, clothes, and furniture. Five or six rooms, so it takes a while to browse.

Island Pursuit. 33rd Street and Long Beach Boulevard, Brant Beach. **(609)494-4944.** Upscale store with a huge selection of casual and sport clothing for men and women. The shop on LBI for

Patagonia, Birkenstock, and Teva sport sandals, shoes, Royal Robbins shorts, Revo shades.

Brant Beach Depot. 62nd Street and Long Beach Boulevard, Brant Beach. (609)361-7790. This wonderful shop has moved around a bit, but it is now permanently installed on 62nd Street. A real emporium in the old sense, with departments stocking antique china and glass, unusual gifts with a seashore motif, paintings, exquisite jewelry, and gourmet foods.

Island Shop. 4205 Long Beach Boulevard, Brant Beach. (609)494-2120. Well-designed men's and women's clothing. About the only place on LBI for women's dressy things. The costume jewelry is gorgeous. So are the sweaters.

Ron Jon's Surf Shop. 8th Street and Central Avenue, Ship Bottom. (609)494-8844. Where surfers or surfer wanna-bes head when they are on the island. All kinds of surfboards and bodyboards plus cool surfing and boarding duds, clothing for men and women made by Quicksilver and Yasa, bathing suits, sunglasses, in-line skates, and lots of gear.

Stutz Candies. 1419 Long Beach Boulevard (at 14th Street), Ship Bottom. (609)494-5303. The traditional stopping-off point to buy your saltwater taffy and fudge before you leave LBI.

Pottery Barge & Gift Shop. 21st Street and Long Beach Boulevard, Ship Bottom. (609)494-0606. When you want off-price china, silverware, or cooking utensils, this is the place. A nice selection of Pfaltzgraff, knives by Sabatier, gadgets by Zyliss, and carving boards, candleholders, glassware, and gifts.

Shoes for U. 24th Street and Long Beach Boulevard, Ship Bottom. (609)494-SHOE. Another location at 110 North Bay Avenue, Beach Haven. (609)492-5490. Discounts run 20 to 50 percent, so come in for a look. Lots of Reebok styles here in running and walking shoes, New Balance, Avia, and Keds. Sperry Topsiders are great for boating and there's Unisa and 9

West when you want to look your best. Neat-looking sandals, purses, and backpacks. The Ship Bottom store has a clearance room for even greater buys.

Gipsy Horse. 8 North Long Beach Boulevard, Surf City. (609)494-8884. Another location at 7 South Bay Avenue, Beach Haven. (609)492-5665. See Lambertville entry for a description. Note: Gipsy Horse has a sensational warehouse sale over Labor Day weekend at the firehouse in Surf City. Everything is in cartons, but prices on J. Crew cottons are next to nothing.

Hill Galleries. 16th Street and Long Beach Boulevard, Surf City. (609)361-8225. A mix of antiques, collectibles, and summer furniture. Lots of outdoor pieces. Some hefty prices, but you can negotiate.

Limited Editions. 22nd Street and Long Beach Boulevard, Surf City. (609)494-0527. One of LBI's top stores for American crafts. Pottery, sculpture, fine jewelry, glass, exciting clothing, and hand-carved wood pieces. The Gull Cottage one-of-a-kind denims for women and children are special.

Long Beach Island Foundation of the Arts and Sciences Gallery. 120 Long Beach Boulevard, Loveladies. (609)494-1241. A lovely place to buy a gift of art, but while you're at it, buy something for yourself. Sophisticated ceramics, painting, and jewelry by some of the East's top artists.

Americana by the Seashore. 604 Broadway, Barnegat Light. (609)494-0656. Antiques, country furniture, quilts, and really nice artificial and dried flowers.

The Sampler. 708 Broadway, Barnegat Light. (609)494-3493. An antique and decorating shop with pillows, chintzes, laces, wall hangings, unusual old toys, and primitives.

The Little Outfit Children's Boutique. 802 Central Avenue, Barnegat Light. (609)494-3622. Really adorable clothes for infants and toddlers.

Brands like Baby Guess, Petit Bateau, and San Francisco City Lights are featured. One of the few places you can buy fancy clothing for children, including christening gowns. The everyday outfits and swimsuits are cute enough to make you melt.

EATS and TASTY TAKEOUT

DiCosmo's. North 6th Street and Long Beach Boulevard, Surf City. (908)361-0064. The first family-run offshoot of the widely known DiCosmo's famous Italian Ices in Elizabeth, NJ, this shop carries all the fresh fruit flavors that the original is known for – luscious lemon, refreshing orange, cherry, and grape. But the stars are the ices made from strawberries, raspberries, and blackberries.

The Dutchman's Brauhaus. 2500 East Bay Avenue (on Cedar Bonnet Island). (609)494-6910. Located at the approach to LBI just after the bridge over Barnegat Bay, the Dutchman affords delightful water views, seafood, and German specialties like sauerbraten and schnitzel. A terrific place for lunch. Hefty portions.

Green Gables Inn. 212 Centre Street, Beach Haven. (609)492-3553. Although dinner here is the most expensive on the island, lunch is affordable and delicious. Imaginative American cuisine, very well prepared. Need an afternoon respite? Do tea with scones and clotted cream. Served until 4 p.m. Get your tea leaves and tarot read on Sundays.

Holiday Snack Bar. Corner of Centre Street and Delaware, Beach Haven. (609)492-4544. Known to cognoscenti, the Holiday is an institution on LBI. Everyone at the counter loves the burgers, but don't eat too much because the desserts are homemade, huge, and delicious.

The Owl Tree. 80th Street and Long Beach Boulevard, Harvey Cedars. (609)494-8191. Their nachos, burgers, salads, fresh seafood make a delightful lunch. Open all year.

Panzone's. Between 11th and 12th on Long Beach Boulevard, Beach Haven. (609)492-5103. Another location at 22nd Street and Long Beach Boulevard, Surf City. (609)494-1114. For the best in pizza, cheesesteaks, and a crowd-pleaser called the Panzoni, a super calzone filled with meats and cheeses. Open year-round, to all hours. Take heart, the line moves very fast!

BEST SHOPPING

BARNEGAT

Babe's In Barnegat. 349 South Main Street (Route 9). (609)698-2223. A large, well-stocked shop devoted to antiques and collectibles. Like most South Jersey shops, this place carries lots of china and smalls. The '40s tablecloths are very nice. Different dealers inside.

Blaze of Glory. 307 South Main Street (Route 9). (609) 660-1464. This two-dealer shop moved over from Manahawkin. Some nice glass, china, and kitchen items.

Gunning River Herbs. 163 Gunning River Road. (609)698-1921. Amazing variety of herbs for your kitchen or for medicinal use, about 75 in all. They advertise "from anise hyssop to yarrow." Try some of the mints in your iced tea. Very interesting shop.

EATS and TASTY TAKEOUT

Dockside Cafe. East Bay Avenue (in the Marina area). (609)698-3010. Watch the boats and dine well. Casual atmosphere.

Hurricane House Restaurant and Ice Cream Parlor. 688 East Bay Avenue. (609)698-7808. This is an authentic ice cream parlor and restaurant dating back to the turn of the century where one can linger in the old wooden booths and soak up the atmosphere. Features Arctic Ice Cream from Trenton and wholesome fare.

 ## BEST SHOPPING

MANAHAWKIN

Manahawkin Mart. 657 East Bay Avenue. **(609)597-1017.** A flea market with 45 indoor shops and outdoor vendors. Open every Saturday and Sunday.

Manor House Shops. 160 North Main Street (Route 9). **(609)597-1122.** Nine individual shops carrying antiques, jewelry, cards, and dried flowers. The painted furniture and folk art are decorative and one shop stocks special occasion apparel.

The Shoppes at Rosewood. 182 North Main Street (Route 9). **(609)597-7331.** A similar concept to Manor House, with nine shops in an impeccably restored Victorian house that dates back to 1890. A little bit of everything – some stunning jewelry and woven cotton summer garments plus a few antiques, scents, and home furnishings.

 ## BEST SHOPPING

TUCKERTON AREA

Tuckerton Emporium. 2 East Main Street (Route 9). **(609)296-2424.** Nine must be a magic number in South Jersey, because Tuckerton Emporium, like other group shops in the region, has nine dealers. There are antiques, a lovely cafe, a clothing boutique, a pottery shop, dried flowers, and jewelry.

ClamTown Books. 1 Shourds Lane (behind H.

G. Marshall & Co). **(609)296-6278.** This is an exciting bookstore that carries lots of local and New Jersey history books plus all the best-sellers, CDs, children's books, jewelry, toys, and gifts.

Old Apple Tree Cottage Shoppes. 130 South Green Street. **(609)294-1527.** An old house packed with antiques, mostly china and glass. Some nice furniture upstairs at Juntiques, Etc., including some furniture from the Arts and Crafts period.

Pine Barrens Antiques. 467 Route 9 South, Eagleswood Township. **(609)597-9300.** Furniture, smalls, painted milk cans.

Shore Craft Tile and Pottery. Route 9 and Cox Lane, West Creek. **(609)296-5480.** Where form and function come together. Earthtone tiles and large practical pieces for the home — bowls, vases, etc. Worth a stop.

 ## EATS and TASTY TAKEOUT

Allen's Clam Bar. Route 9 at New York Road, New Gretna. **(609)296-4106.** The clam fritters are tasty and filled with just-shucked mollusks. Clam chowder and oyster stew are a few of the delicious specialties. People head here from LBI and Atlantic City.

 # WORTH a DETOUR
OCEANVILLE

This is what the Jersey Shore towns used to look like before superhighways, casinos, and fast food eateries. The Noyes Museum, Route 9 and Lily Lake Road, (609)652-8848, is known for its fabulous bird decoys that were collected by the Noyes family. This private museum shows the work of contemporary carvers, pottery, and photography. Open Wednesday through Sunday from 11 a.m. to 4 p.m. At the Edwin B. Forsythe National Wildlife Refuge, Lily Lake Road (beyond

Noyes Museum), (609)652-1665, visitors can access thousands of acres of tidal marshes that support bird and marine wildlife. There's an 8-mile dirt road that winds through the refuge. Stop anywhere. Open sunrise to sunset. $4 entry per car.

Directions: *From Tuckerton,* follow Route 9 south (the highway merges into the Garden State Parkway for three miles and becomes a separate road again). Oceanville is 6 miles after the Bass River marinas.

Seafarer Ltd. **Route 9 and Lily Lake Road. (609)652-9491.** A 3,000-square-foot shop devoted to nautical decor and antiques. Lovely furniture, lots of copper and brass.

SMITHVILLE

Directions: From Tuckerton, follow Route 9 south (the highway merges into the Garden State Parkway for three miles and becomes a separate road again). Smithville is about 3 miles after the Bass River marinas.

Historic Towne of Smithville. **Route 9. (609)652-7777.** Smithville is a restored colonial village built around a lovely inland lake. It has specialty shops, antique shops, crafts stores, and restaurants — all linked by cobblestone paths.

SHORTER SHOPPING TRIPS in SOUTHERN NEW JERSEY

GREENWICH

Pronounced "Gren-itch," this historic village on the banks of the scenic Cohansey River has a wealth of preserved 18th-century architecture. Visitors find the area more evocative of Maryland's Eastern Shore than of the New Jersey. There's an old tavern, a schoolhouse, and a maritime museum on Bacon's Neck Road, open summers only. The Cumberland County Historic Society operates the circa 1730 Gibbon House on Main Street as a museum.

Directions: Take Route 295 South toward the Delaware Memorial Bridge. Get off at Route 551 heading toward Salem. At Salem, pick up Route 49 East toward Bridgeton and go 12 miles to Shiloh. At the blinker light in Shiloh, make a sharp right onto Route 620 and go through Roadstown into Greenwich. When you reach Route 623, turn left to reach the center of the historic village. Turn right on Johnson Avenue to reach the river. From Route 523, turn right to get to Sheppards Mill Road and the shops there.

 **BEST SHOPPING**

Shiloh Antiques. South Main Street (Route 49), Shiloh. (609)453-1800. At the blinker light on the left in Shiloh Village. Period pieces to primitives in this group shop. Open 10 a.m. to 5 p.m. Thursday to Sunday and other days by chance.

Robert W. Green Antiques. Roadstown-Greenwich Road (at Route 626). (609)451-4256. Everything in this shop has exceptional quality and age, with most pieces in the original paint or stain. Open Sundays.

The Griffin. Piney Mount Run and Sheppards Mill Road. (609)451-8454. Antiques, gifts, and out-of-print books. Open Wednesday to Sunday, April through December.

 EATS and TASTY TAKEOUT

Ship John Inn. Pier and Market streets (on the Cohansey). (609)451-1444. Fine dining. Open for lunch and dinner but closed Monday and Tuesday.

HADDONFIELD

Haddonfield's historic district encompasses more than 400 colonial and Victorian period buildings. The town was settled by Quakers in 1682. It is charming, with unusual shops, cafes, and brick plazas. Indian King Tavern at 233 King's Highway East, (609)429-6792, is a state-operated museum open Wednesday through Sunday. It closes for lunch.

Directions: Turn off Route 70 in Cherry Hill onto King's Highway (Route 41) and go south a little more than 1 mile to Haddonfield.

 **BEST SHOPPING**

Omaha Steaks. 49 King's Highway East. **(609)427-4496.** Premium cornfed Midwestern beef is sold here in packages, aged, trimmed, and frozen. The store, the first in New Jersey for the chain, is attractively decorated, with freezers lining one wall. Shoppers can also purchase chicken. Barbecue tools and sauces from El Paso Chile Co. are available as well.

Yvonne O'Gara Collections. 55 King's Highway East. **(609)429-7117.** Beautifully appointed home furnishings shop with over-stuffed furniture, frames, and interesting pillows and accessories.

Primadonna. 57 King's Highway East. **(609)354-1696.** Casual clothing store for women, with No Saint and other easy-to-wear jackets, pants with elastic waists, and skirts in longer lengths. Handsome accessories.

One World. 105 King's Highway East. **(609)429-4200.** A store for environmentally sensitive products and gifts, such as cotton-fiber clothing, sponges, earthenware pottery, and soaps. Form is not sacrificed for function at One World.

Au Courant. 106 King's Highway East. **(609)546-3051.** One of the best women's shops in South Jersey, Au Courant carries high-fashion suits, blazers, and skirts.

Picadilly Circus, Ltd. 113 King's Highway East. **(609)216-0192.** This shop bills its clothes as kids' couture and this moniker is about right — the clothes are gorgeous and expensive. Items in bright-colored soft fleece for infants and toddlers.

Gipsy Horse. 139 King's Highway East. (609)428-6262. See entry under Lambertville for a description. Note: the Haddonfield store is one of the chain's best.

The Owl's Tale. 140 King's Highway East. (609)795-8110. Large antique Specializes in old silver, some Art Nouveau, china, and estate jewelry. On a recent visit, there was a lot of nice Roseville. Sales personnel are very knowledgeable.

Cronin & Murphy Antiques. 13 South Haddon Avenue (coming into town from Route 70, turn left on Haddon Avenue). (609)428-8833. Dealers specialize in the Arts and Crafts period. Mission furniture and art pottery are among the best things in the shop.

 EATS and TASTY TAKEOUT

La Patisserie Francaise. 101 Ellis Street (at Haddon Avenue). (609)428-0418. The croissants are to die for and so are the butter cakes and cookies. Eat in or take out.

Remi's Cafe. 141 King's Highway East. (609)795-7232. A great spot for lunch with an Italian-flavored menu but with hamburgers and salads, too.

MULLICA HILL

Tucked away in South Jersey near the Delaware River Memorial Bridge, Mullica Hill has become a major antique center. Its colonial and Victorian homes along Main Street house dozens of antique shops, all within a half-mile stretch. Most are open Wednesday through Sunday. Merchants put on a number of special events, such as Fall Open House, which combines shopping with Civil War re-creation activities. Knowledgeable antiquers make this a regular stop on the Washington, D.C., to New York run.

Directions: Mullica Hill is at the junction of Routes 322 and 45. Take the New Jersey Turnpike, Exit 2, to Route 322 and go 3 miles into Mullica Hill. Turn right at the traffic light. Or take Route 295, get off at Exit 11 (Route 45) and head south 9 miles.

 **BEST SHOPPING**

Old Mill Antique Mall. 1 South Main Street. **(609)478-9810.** Three floors of antiques — china, vintage clothing, postcards, and smalls in lighted cases. About 40 dealers.

Antiquities at Mullica Hill. 43 South Main Street. **(609)478-6773.** Elegant formal furniture of the 18th and 19th centuries, some country furniture, paintings, and lots of Chinese porcelains and Imari.

Lynne Antiques. 49 South Main Street. **(609)223-9199.** This is a good shop with quality smalls and some desirable furniture.

The Yellow Garage Antiques. 66 South Main Street. **(609)478-0300.** Proprietors Tracy Dodge and Steven Lipman have turned an old garage into a high-quality group shop. Primitives, folk art, country furniture, wicker, collectibles from the '40s.

Raccoon's Tale. 6 High Street. **(609)478-4488.** Owner Ed Stump has the finest Fiestaware, Lu-Ray, Russel Wright, and Harlequin in New Jersey! Add to your set or buy a whole new set for your kitchen.

EATS and TASTY TAKEOUT

Hilltop Restaurant. 47 South Main Street. **(609)478-2112.** Plain fare, in the middle of the antique district.

WOODSTOWN

Woodstown is an unexpected visual delight. Ride through the principal thoroughfare of this Delaware River town, and you might think you were in the early 18th century. Brick townhouses dating back to that time line the avenue like sentries.

Directions: *From New Jersey Turnpike,* get off at Exit 1. Follow U.S. Route 40 East about 6 miles. Best Shopping

 **BEST SHOPPING**

Cowtown Flea Market. U.S. Route 40. **(609)769-3200.** Every Tuesday and Saturday all year, between 650 and 700 dealers in antiques and collectibles gather on the grounds of New Jersey's only professional rodeo. This is the market's 52nd year! The best buys are the kitchenware from the '30s and '40s, including the reticulated Bauer bowls that Martha Stewart loves so much. However, collectors of all types of antiques will have a field day here. Hours are 8 a.m. to 4 p.m. Many weekend browsers stay for the rodeo, which runs every Saturday from Memorial Day to the end of September.

Index

Antiques